Martin Wainwright is Northern Editor of the *Guardian*, author of *The Guardian Book of April Fool's Day* and *The Coast-to-Coast Walk* and editor of *A Lifetime of Mountains: The Best of A. Harry Griffin's Country Diary*, all published by Aurum. His new book for Aurum is *Morris Minor: The Biography. Sixty Years of Britain's Favourite Car.*

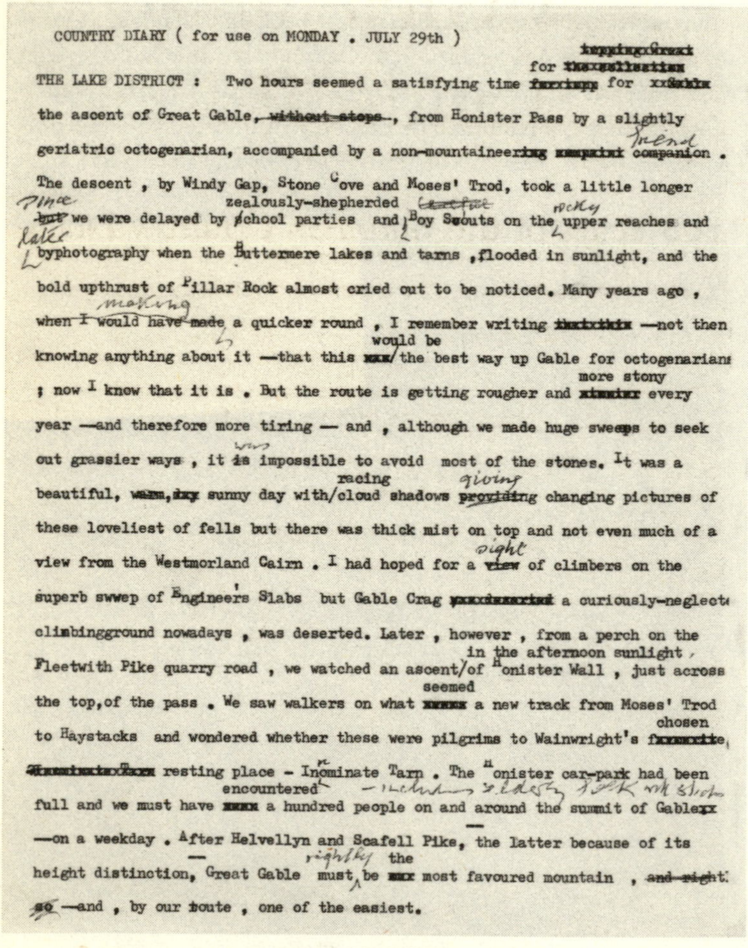

COUNTRY DIARY (for use on MONDAY . JULY 29th)

THE LAKE DISTRICT : Two hours seemed a satisfying time for the ascent of Great Gable, ~~without stops~~, from Honister Pass by a slightly geriatric octogenarian, accompanied by a non-mountaineering friend ~~companion~~. The descent , by Windy Gap, Stone Cove and Moses' Trod, took a little longer since ~~but~~ we were delayed by zealously-shepherded school parties and Boy Scouts on the rocky upper reaches and later by photography when the Buttermere lakes and tarns ,flooded in sunlight, and the bold upthrust of Pillar Rock almost cried out to be noticed. Many years ago , when ~~I would have made~~ making a quicker round , I remember writing —not then knowing anything about it —that this would be the best way up Gable for octogenarians ; now I know that it is . But the route is getting rougher and more stony every year —and therefore more tiring — and , although we made huge sweeps to seek out grassier ways , it ~~is~~ was impossible to avoid most of the stones. It was a beautiful, sunny day with racing cloud shadows ~~providing~~ giving changing pictures of these loveliest of fells but there was thick mist on top and not even much of a view from the Westmorland Cairn . I had hoped for a ~~view~~ sight of climbers on the superb swwep of Engineer's Slabs but Gable Crag a curiously-neglected climbingground nowadays , was deserted. Later , however , from a perch on the Fleetwith Pike quarry road , we watched an ascent in the afternoon sunlight, of Honister Wall , just across the top of the pass . We saw walkers on what seemed a new track from Moses' Trod to Haystacks and wondered whether these were pilgrims to Wainwright's chosen resting place - Innominate Tarn . The Honister car-park had been full and we must have encountered – including elderly folk with sticks – a hundred people on and around the summit of Gable —on a weekday . After Helvellyn and Scafell Pike, — the latter because of its height distinction, — Great Gable must rightly be the most favoured mountain , ~~and rightly so~~ —and , by our route , one of the easiest.

A perfectionist – Harry Griffin cut his typing paper to meet exactly the diary's word length and then sprinkled the script with afterthoughts

A Gleaming Landscape

100 Years of the *Guardian* Country Diary

Edited

by Martin Wainwright

Illustrations

by Clifford Harper

theguardian

Aurum

First published 2006 by
Aurum Press Ltd, 7 Greenland Street London NW1 0ND
www.aurumpress.co.uk
in association with Guardian Books.
Guardian Books is an imprint of Guardian Newspapers Ltd
This paperback edition first published in 2008 by Aurum Press

The Country Diary pieces collected in this book were
first published in the *Guardian*.

Photo credits: p. 13 Arnold Boyd and Thomas Coward: Eric Hosking Trust; p. 29 Helena
Swanwick: Mary Evans Picture Library; p. 71 Arnold Boyd: Eric Hosking Trust; p. 109
Harry Griffin: Denis Thorpe, Guardian Newspapers; p. 125 Enid Wilson: Don McPhee,
Guardian Newspapers; p. 129 William Condry: Denis Thorpe, Guardian Newspapers;
p. 153 Diarists' lunch: courtesy of Guardian Newspapers; p. 183 Pete Postance: courtesy
of Guardian Newspapers; p. 199 Ted Ellis: courtesy of the Wolf Brewery;
p. 213 Pete Bowler: Denis Thorpe, Guardian Newspapers

A catalogue record for this book is available from the British Library.

ISBN 978 1 84513 368 9

1 3 5 7 9 10 8 6 4 2
2008 2010 2012 2011 2009

Designed in Perpetua by Peter Ward
Typeset by M Rules
Printed in the UK by CPI Bookmarque, Croydon, CR0 4TD

'Suddenly, a shaft of sunlight seeded the rushes with diamonds, the whole landscape gleamed.'

Jim Perrin, Country Diary, December 2005

Country diary

Lake District

I have been taken to task by a reader from Hampshire who, quite rightly, points out my erroneous description of the electrifying rollercoaster of the Buttermere "round" as starting with Red Pike and finishing with Robinson. As David Ross, a retired buyer in local government, says, "This is, of course, a mere half round."

It was in the early 60s, he relates, when the then proprietor of the Bridge Hotel in Buttermere, the much-loved Rodney Twitchin, offered a prize of a bottle of champagne to the guest or member of staff who could complete the round in the fastest time. This started and finished in the bar of the Bridge and involved traversing the summits of Whiteless Pike, Wandope, Grasmoor, Hobcarton Pike, Whiteside, Mellbreak, Red Pike, High Stile, High Crag, Haystacks, Fleetwith Pike, Dalehead, Hindscarth and Robinson, a walk of some 30 miles with an ascent (and descent) of over 10,000ft.

During a spell as a handyman at the Bridge, he completed the round on his day off in seven hours and 39 minutes, aided by a cache of Mars Bars at Scarth Gap. "Rodney," he says, "declared this was worthy of a magnum of champagne, but then found he had no magnum in stock so brought out a jeroboam of the finest vintage – typical of the man. This was consumed with great enjoyment by guests and staff alike, all piled into the tiny bar." The empty bottle, a prized trophy, still sits in the living room of the house he shares with the woman he first met in that "wonderful establishment", the Bridge Hotel. Some 27 years later he "foolishly" decided to repeat the round. "It took 12 and a half exhausting hours, with no champagne to revive me," he recalls. It is not surprising David Ross still regards the Buttermere valley as a piece of heaven on earth.
Tony Greenbank

Readers' suggestions and sometimes corrections have always given diarists fresh material, from the earliest days to this entry by Tony Greenbank in June 2006

Contents

INTRODUCTION

When I started scrolling through the microfilms which open the door to a hundred years of the *Guardian*'s Country Diary, I had no idea that I was going to discover a writer who did battle against satanists or a printer who stepped in with one of his fishing stories when the regular contributor's copy got lost. Working through the reels, I found another diarist who taught Virgina Woolf Greek and, according to the novelist, 'gaped like a benevolent gudgeon' when she was told before anyone else about the teenage Woolf's sexual abuse by a stepbrother. Such people added perspective to more predictable although appealing naturalists, Harry Tegner dashing to reach a dead, beached shark before the council binmen, Bill Campbell waking neighbours at midnight to show them his captured glow-worm (peering through their windows lit only by the ghostly greenish light).

Such experiences were useful beyond the pleasure of wondering: whatever next? Because this was like being a Country Diarist myself, exploring a landscape which appeared to be peaceful – Leeds reference library or the John Rylands special collections at Manchester University – and then, whoosh! up started the equivalent of the great crested grebe or spider or eel which gave these writers their 300 words for the week. And what powerful words. The Country Diary is small but has always attracted an enormous correspondence, and a fascination, expressed in thousands of letters in the personal archives of the diarists, as to who these invisible friends in the countryside might be.

Second only to Araucaria, the monkey-puzzler Revd John Graham who still compiles his crossword at the age of 86, the diarists crop up most frequently when I meet regular *Guardian* readers. Did I know Harry Griffin, Enid Wilson or Pete Bowler? Do I see Paul Evans or Sarah Poyntz? None of these are 'star' writers with picture bylines, but they have helped to build a national institution over 103 years. That gives them a claim to run the longest-lasting uninterrupted column in British newspapers, although it is part of the endearing history of Country Diarists that this claim has to fail. Not many people know this – in fact I am the only living one who does until now – but on 19 January 1925 the art and literary critic Basil de Selincourt wrote to the *Guardian*'s famous editor C.P. Scott: 'I am so very sorry and ashamed to have failed you with my CD [Country Diary] lately. Last Monday when I should have sent it off, I was very busy and forgot.' That is why there was nothing that Wednesday between The Weather and Cyclists' Lamping Up Time.

It is timely that the diary is now enjoying a renaissance in the *Guardian*'s latest reinvention of itself. As an occasional leader-writer, I was present when the editor Alan Rusbridger unveiled dummies of the leader page, the most prestigious in the paper, during the count-down to the 2005 redesign. What was I seeing? Good heavens, the Country Diary was there, next to the leaders and Corrections and Clarifications. I had just been compiling a collection of diaries by Harry Griffin, the doyen of the writers who continued until he died at the age of 93 in 2004. 'I know someone who will be happy,' I said, pointing skywards, where Harry would have been telling other angels how awful it was when the diary was exiled from the leader page in the 1980s. 'That makes two of us,' said Alan, who had persuaded hard-nosed colleagues to allow such ephemera this honoured slot.

But then, the diary isn't ephemeral. Most journalism is (the word means 'of the day' and no one has achieved lasting fame through journalism alone); but the Country Diaries have lasted because they are such good natural history observation written for the most part with flair. Many diarists have published their own collections and almost all have written books on their specialist fields: 25 in Harry Griffin's case, 35 in Elliot Grant Watson's and more than 40 in Tegner's, including my favourite title: *Beasts of the North Country: from Whales to Shrews*. They are true heirs to their inspiration the Revd Gilbert White, whose *Natural History of Selborne* has not been out of print since it was published in 1789. The date is significant: the French Revolution, the Americans newly on their own feet. But White's first readers also wanted to spend time with a vicar in his Hampshire garden, pondering why worms are so 'much addicted to venery' and following the meanderings of Timothy, his aunt's tortoise.

The subject is everything. The British countryside is varied and lovely. No two days of weather are the same. British beasts and birds are fascinating, down to the 38 species of woodlouse which caused one of the biggest debates in the Diary's history (about whether they roll up or not when touched). This is a more fundamental world than goings-on in Whitehall or Baghdad, and not just as a calmer, sweeter alternative. The countryside is the frontier where Nature fights against exploitation, ultimately for our survival. Like scouts, the diarists bring back reports on the struggle, all the more effectively because like White, who discovered three native species including the harvest mouse, they know what they are writing about.

Finally it is important that they are journalists, either by profession or adoption. There is much wrong with our lickety-split trade, but its virtue is making complicated matters accessible to busy readers. I still get a compulsion to read on from an intro such as Pete

Bowler's 'The emergence of newts from their winter hibernation tends to go unremarked.' Or this one from Arnold Boyd, whose book *A Country Parish* is Cheshire's *Selborne*: 'I cannot help thinking that if only Hitler had been an ornithologist, he would have put off the war until the autumn bird migration was over.' Whimsical but written in the darkness of 1939, it helps explain why Britain won.

The diaries are in chronological order in the hope that this is the easiest way to cope with a century, apart from a few Then as Nows where a later diarist has chosen exactly the same theme. There is an entry for every year and from every writer I have been able to identify, including Peter Postance, the printer who filled the gap when a diary got lost in the early days of electronic inputting. If any reader can identify MA or CHDA, who remain mysteries to me, I would be delighted. I am very grateful to Dr James Peters at the John Rylands library, Martin Lambert of Doncaster Museum, Tony Usher of Knutsford Ornithological Society, Gavin McGuffie at the *Guardian*'s Newsroom archive and Richard Neilsson and Katy Heslop at the paper's research department, and to all their unfailingly helpful and cheerful colleagues. Thanks also to Celia Locks who edited the Country Diary, her successor Jeannette Page, Manchester and Leeds reference libraries and, of course, Google. It has been a pleasure working with Lisa Darnell and Ben Siegle of Guardian Books and Graham Coster and Phoebe Clapham at Aurum Press. And now, before we go back to 1904 and the bustle of Manchester, here is a November entry from William Condry, a contributor for 30 years, which answers a question you may be asking . . .

What use old diaries?
NOVEMBER 1974

Naturalists are sometimes great diarists. Or if not great they are persistent. For maybe sixty years a chap will write down a daily miscellany of what seem rather pointless observations about plants, birds, mammals, insects, fish or merely the weather, pointless because he hardly ever refers to them again. Never mind, diary-keeping amuses him and does no harm. And it's always possible that when he dies his journals will get preserved in a library somewhere. There they may lie neglected for half a century but eventually some-body feels inquisitive enough to dip into them. The dross of fifty years ago, like old bottles, has acquired an unexpected value. These thoughts occur to me because I am just now reading the life-long diaries of a local naturalist who flourished earlier this century. J.H. Salter, professor of botany at Aberystwyth, was a true all-rounder. Wandering the lanes and woods he identified birds, reptiles, mam-mals, moths and beetles just as easily as plants. For many of these species there has been little change since his day. But some have gone. The corn buntings, woodlarks, shrikes and some of the plants he mentions are not of our time. The world of nature he knew already seems a little unreal and will be even more interesting to readers fifty years from now. So, gathering his little daily store of notes, our diarist, without realising it, was writing a quite unique kind of history.

William Condry

CHAPTER ONE

Origin of the Species

The first nature notes on the *Guardian*'s patch were kept in the 1670s by Manchester's churchwardens, who were responsible for public health and did their work with Old Testament zeal. They left a record of shilling bounties paid for dead foxes, badgers, otters and other 'vermin' which forms an unintentional but interesting species distribution chart; 96 hedgehogs, for example, were caught in 1674. Private journals from the same era add colour. A Crosby merchant called Nicholas Blundell counted and destroyed crows' nests – 94 one year, two the next – before observing his family with other animals: 'Fanny had one of her violent Convulsion Fits, it being occasioned by seeing a Mous in her Roome.'

Such a mixture of fact and fun is the lifeblood of journalism, and when the *Manchester Guardian* began in 1821, its founders lightened the commercial and political ballast with similar natural history records and anecdote. A page-long column called Farm Notes appeared irregularly; the Hon. R.C. Drummond wrote from time to time about fish. For the rest of the century such material was used in the characteristically disorganised way of daily newspapers. But by the late 1890s, intense commercial rivalry was concentrating editors' and proprietors' minds. It was in these circumstances that the *Guardian*'s Country Diary was born.

Its debut on 21 March 1904 came at a time of particular crisis for the newspaper. The long-standing owner John Edward Taylor was 74 and his health was broken; he was to die the following year. His first cousin C.P. Scott, the paper's editor who was to become the greatest figure in the *Guardian*'s history, seems with hindsight the obvious successor as owner, but he had to fight ruthless internal opponents for a long time. Meanwhile the Harmsworths had arrived in Manchester to launch a *Northern Daily Mail*; so had the *Sunday Chronicle* run by Edward Hulton, who had been sacked as a young man by the *Guardian* for plagiarising sports results for his freelance sheet *Prophetic Notes*. The *Guardian*'s local monopoly of fine writing was threatened by such columns as the *Chronicle*'s Babble from Babylon, written by a London insider called The Bounder whose style Manchester journalists admired.

The newcomers were pitching at young, demanding readers, the first generation to grow up after the 1870 Education Act. A typesetter at the *Guardian* told Scott that ordinary people found too little of general interest in the paper. Senior journalists were saying the same thing. The result was a flurry of special features such as Cycling Notes to keep pace with a craze as consuming as today's iPods, and soon afterwards a sister column called Automobiles. Miscellany, a counter to Babble which became one of the *Guardian*'s longest-lasting features, started in 1903. And then, in January 1904, a letter arrived at the home in Cheshire of a retired textile dyer and bleacher called Thomas Coward who was, to put it mildly, fanatical about birds.

It came from a man known in Manchester's cosy business world as 'Sider', Herbert Sidebotham, a senior lieutenant of Scott's who made it his business to squirrel out interesting characters in the north-west. He had heard a lot about Coward: how he believed in identifying rare birds and animals by their 'jizz', a Cheshire word derived from 'guise' and meaning small peculiarities or habits; and the way he sat at the end of the pew in church, to be able to nip out when services were interrupted by the song of an interesting bird. Coward had also written a couple of readable books but – a key piece of information picked up by Sider – was having to live on limited income from a golden handshake when his company was taken over by the Bleachers' Combine. Sider offered him five shillings a day to 'contribute daily one or two articles on country life'.

This was £150 a week in today's money and John Edward Taylor was concerned when he heard about it. He monitored the paper closely; day by day, his handwritten letters arrived at Cross Street in Manchester from his home in Kensington Palace Gardens – London's 'Millionaires' Row' – or convalescent hotels in Eastbourne and Tunbridge Wells. Was a third leader on trousers which referred to 'natural bulges' really something which should appear in the *Manchester Guardian*? (No, sorry, acknowledged its writer, the paper's star essayist C.E. Montague.) Taylor thought that the new feature, called Country Lover's Diary for its first two years, was a good idea, but surely hard to keep going all year round?

Sider and Scott had no such doubts. Quite apart from the interest of birds, animals and flowers, the countryside was particularly rich in the issues the paper liked to explore. It was also undergoing momentous change. A series called 'Rambles around Manchester' in the *Guardian* had attracted much correspondence over its graphic description of half-derelict villages looking 'as if they had been sacked by a hostile army' after the collapse of the coach trade in the face of railway competition. The day of the car was meanwhile starting to dawn. The two men also had enough faith in Coward to give him a monopoly. Initially they had wondered about alternating him with another 'skilful paragraphist', as Taylor put it in a good précis of Country Diarists' essential qualification. But Coward persuaded them that the column would be more coherent if it came from a single hand, particularly as he had strong views on farming and conservation which others might not share. He was also understandably keen on thirty shillings a week. 'If you decide to give me a daily space,' he wrote to Sidebotham, 'I should much prefer to have it to myself.'

It was a demanding brief compared with Country Diary routine in years to come, when regular writers were to contribute weekly, fortnightly or sometimes just once a month. There were times when the paper seemed to be running a Cheshire Country Lover's Diary. Coward lived in the county all his life and the book which began his reputation, in 1900, was *The Birds of Cheshire*. It was not until 1920 that he published the definitive *The Birds of the British Isles and Their Eggs*, one of the best books ever written on the subject and never matched in terms of making ornithology a mass hobby. The fact that the Royal Society for the Protection of Birds – founded in 1889 – now has over a million members is partly owing to Coward, who was one of the first.

But he was also one of the most skilled all-round field naturalists Britain has produced; even in 1932, the year before his death, his diary listed ten lecture engagements on subjects including Birds and Insects, Episodes of Animal Life, and Whales and Whaling, in addition to BBC countryside radio broadcasts, for he was by then a national name. The trenchant views which he did not want diluted by alternative voices in the Country Diary could be reproduced unaltered today. He wrote: 'We must maintain balance because if we do not, we as well as the lower animals will suffer. It is with this end in mind that economic zoology and botany should be studied.' And: 'Too late the public conscience awakes to the fact that the presence of open space means more than sentiment.' His 50 years of meticulous bird records are used today as important indicators of climate change.

His *Guardian* diary was an immediate success, particularly in the way that it became a readers' club, for Coward was in touch with hundreds of naturalists, many of them uneducated but skilled observers while others were poachers or the last of the Smallweed-like rarity collectors who had flourished in Victorian times. Scores of his entries end with mysterious notes such as (on 1 December 1906): 'J.T. Thanks for letter. Not very exceptional in gardens at this season.' He often based diaries on correspondents' questions about everything from spiders to weather records, and made unashamed but always attributed use of others' observations. This became a Country Diary tradition.

In 1909 Scott sent Coward a note praising the column but wondering: 'Would you care to have a little relief, say on two days a week?' Perhaps someone else might offer a slightly more varied set of insights, on the condition of farming or gardening? This is the first example of another lasting theme of the Country Diary: editor after editor worried that there might be too much about birds. When Harry Griffin, the longest-serving of all diarists with 53 years in the job, was appointed in 1952, he was told by Scott's successor A.P. Wadsworth: 'For God's sake keep off birds. We get enough of them from the others.' One of the most popular of all the writers, Arnold Boyd, admitted in a diary in 1942: 'A Cheshire country diarist may weary his readers by frequent mention of great crested grebes.' A year later Boyd's editor William Crozier encouraged another diarist, J.K. Adams, to try writing the odd third leader on birds, but cautioned: 'one mustn't overdo them because of the attention they get in the Diary'.

Coward's column, usually 250 words on the back page, had started with plenty of variety: chickweed, frogspawn, rats, gnats and an otter in its first week. But he admitted in reply to Scott that his column 'sometimes ran in one direction', partly because so many of his correspondents shared his interest in birds. He managed to fend off collaboration for the time being, for the most pressing of reasons. 'To be perfectly honest I have to consider the pay. Four days a week would mean a pound instead of 30 shillings and so long as you are willing to pay me that, I do not feel I can afford to let it go.' He added in the best freelance tradition that his work had attracted interest from the *Scotsman* and London papers.

Scott let matters lie but repeated his hopes for more range even though 'I like the birds because you write so interestingly about them.' Four years later he moved more firmly. Coward was given a signed column (only the initials TAC but that was fame in those days) in exchange for writing on Monday, Wednesday and Friday, while a new hand took Tuesday, Thursday and Saturday. He replied sadly from Devon where he was nursing his invalid wife that he would feel the loss of 15 shillings a week. But he made a significant concession: 'The daily preparation of a paragraph has not always been easy, especially during slack seasons; I admit that it will often be a relief to have only three a week to think about.' Taylor must have smiled from his grave.

Grebes from the start — the first entry
~ MARCH 1904 ~

The mallards which through the winter have been spending their days on the Cheshire mere, have at last departed. Only a few pairs of birds which nest in the covets near the water now remain; we miss the sonorous quacks and contented chuckles. A few diving ducks are still on the waters, and more will come, remain a few days and then pass on to the northward. The grebes, gay in their nuptial plumes, and the lumbering coots are left in possession of the meres. Today the grebes were performing their strange pairing antics, stretching their long necks and fencing with one another's bills, spreading the while their fine chestnut tippets to their full extent. A curlew flew over, calling as it passed; doubtless it was travelling from the coast mudflats to its breeding ground on the high moors of the Derbyshire border. The strange drumming of the snipe is a note of spring; it may be heard now on the moors or on the flat, boggy land. It is supposed to be caused by the rush of air through the stiff tail feathers when the snipe makes a sudden descent, and it sounds uncommonly like a lamb bleating in the air above our heads.

Thomas Coward

Rabbit versus stoats
⟳ JULY 1905 ⟲

The families of stoats, even when the young are well advanced, keep together and hunt in packs. A friend who was walking along the river Lune witnessed a few days ago a most interesting incident. All at once the bank near to him, which rose somewhat sharply, seemed to be alive with stoats, for though he estimated that there were only six or seven their quick movements made their numbers appear to be greater. They made for a heap of stones, probably their home, and then, like a lot of kittens, began to play, tumbling over one another and rolling down the bank or chasing their comrades' tails. On the top of the bank was an old buck rabbit, evidently watching his natural foes. Suddenly, without any warning, 'he came like an old cart horse at full gallop' down the bank at two of the youngsters which had strayed a distance from the stones. Scared, they bolted for home. Immediately afterwards the rabbit saw another one and, running at it, bowled it clean over, making it scream with fear. Then the rabbit returned to the top of the bank and stood on guard, but he did not again attack the stoats, for the lively little creatures wisely kept to the heap of stones for their play. The rabbit was in no way threatened by the stoats, the assault was altogether unprovoked; perhaps, however, he had former murders to avenge. At times the timid rabbit can show plenty of pluck.

Thomas Coward

*Men of Cheshire: Thomas Coward (right) and his successor as
diarist Arnold Boyd, by one of their favourite meres*

Then as now 1

SEPTEMBER 1939

The tumblings and curvetings in which a stoat occasionally indulges (about which 'FC' of Oldham inquires) are undoubtedly a very powerful attraction to birds. It is supposed that the stoat performs these antics so as to bring the bird within range, but often enough they appear to be purely the outcome of joie de vivre. Apparently the stoat he watched made no real attempt to capture the wheatear which fluttered near it. I once saw a stoat running in circles in my garden; a blackbird, a thrush, a starling, two blue tits and six sparrows lined up to watch the show, but on none was any attack made. Again, during a fight between a stoat and a rat which I watched in a country lane the ringside seats were occupied by a great tit, two yellowhammers and four sparrows; one sparrow was so greatly interested that it hopped within a foot of the dying rat when the stoat finally left it, and really inspected it.

Arnold Boyd

Then as now 2

JUNE 1973

Recently I mentioned a pair of stoats that were visiting our bird table near Machynlleth. Since then we have seen them regularly and have been able to learn something about their food preferences. By long tradition stoats are invariably portrayed as bloodthirsty. But, from what I have seen lately, I would say that they will sample pretty well everything, and are very happy to settle for meat and two vegetables at lunch-time which is when they always appear at our bird table. Yesterday there was a strange episode. One of the stoats appeared to go quite berserk, dashing all over the lawn at a tremendous rate in a series of wild zigzags. Then he executed a succession of forward gambols at the same breakneck speed. Things got even wilder when he leapt high into the air several times, landing flat on his back but immediately raced on again. I soon realised that I was witnessing the famous dancing of the stoat, a stunt by which rabbits and birds are supposed to be so fascinated that they venture very close out of curiosity. The crafty stoat, so the tale goes, then suddenly leaps out and seizes the victim from among the circle of bewitched spectators. I have always put this story firmly among those about shaggy dogs and now that I have seen the act for myself I am even more sceptical. For no rabbits or birds arrived as witnesses and I would have sworn that the stoat, far from playing a clever part, was in reality having some sort of a fit. So I prefer to believe that stoats suffer from a strange nervous disorder that causes these outlandish performances.

William Condry

Then as now 3
DECEMBER 2001

If there had not been a long gap between the alders lining the burn near Strathnairn I would not have been able to focus my binoculars on the stoat. It was bounding along above the burn in what looked like sheer ecstasy, with its black-tipped tail waving as if in display. At the other end was a woodmouse in the stoat's jaws, and its long thin tail was also waving.

The surprise was that in the latter part of December and this far north the stoat was still brown and not in its white winter coat. It was thought at one time that the change was linked to temperature, so that in a mild winter some individuals did not change. Research has indicated that not only temperature but also heredity is a factor, with some stoats never changing to white.

The stoat's visibility can be contrasted with the pine marten, which mainly kills at night. There are exceptions to this such as in very poor weather or when the young are being fed, and then daylight raids by pine martens have been seen. But the stoat, being much smaller, has to take smaller prey more often, so has to hunt by day and by night. It seems that in this strath it is the larger male stoat that will tackle poultry such as hens and ducks, while the smaller female goes for the eggs.

At one stage we were losing four or five hen's eggs a day. We just thought the birds were having a quiet patch, until I found some egg yolk outside a hutch where an egg had been broken. Then the next day I saw the female stoat rolling an egg away by pushing it with her nose. Whether you find stoats attractive or admire their frenzied lifestyle in which they hypnotise rabbits probably depends on whether you keep poultry.

Ray Collier

Holiday weather
❧ AUGUST 1905 ❧

Holiday-makers who today must return to town may be excused if they grumble a little. The sun was shining brightly when trainloads of people were hurrying back to work. The farmer as well as the holiday-maker found the heavy rain of yesterday a little trying. Much of his corn was already badly laid, and the heavy thunder showers beat it down still more. In Cheshire many fields of oats have been cut early, but there are many more untouched; it makes one sad to look at the ripening wheat, flat as if a roller had passed over it; the promised early harvest will be a laborious one. Sparrows are holding high festival in the corn; for them it is a time of riot and feasting. Some are still feeding young in the nest, and we hope feeding them on noxious grubs, but large numbers have deserted for a time the habitations of man, only, however, to take their young to his cultivated fields. I saw a boy walking round one field with the old-fashioned clappers. When he approached the sparrows rose in a cloud and flew; but they departed from the edge of the field to drop near the middle, so the clapper was not much use.

Thomas Coward

Don't pick the flowers
APRIL 1906

The black poplar, its widespread branches thickly hung with deep red male catkins, is one of the most striking of the trees at present, especially when the sunlight falls upon it; those who, these holidays, have wandered through our Cheshire lanes must have noticed the warm glow on these trees contrasting with the vivid green of young leaves on other trees and bushes. Yesterday, in one of the few remaining spots in this neighbourhood where they have not been discovered by root-grubbers, I found a few sweet violets in flower; they appear annually within ten miles of the [Manchester] Town Hall.

For some time I have been watching the evolutions of a pair of kestrels which have apparently selected a particular wood for their domestic operations and perhaps have even chosen and are using a nesting site – very likely the old nest of some other bird. The pair used daily to wheel high above the trees in circles, crossing and re-crossing each other's track, but during the last few days I have only noticed the male. A kestrel, by the way, was on Saturday hovering above the gardens in Bowdon, but I did not see it drop upon any unsuspecting mice. It is not common to see this useful bird hunting over a garden.

Thomas Coward

Birds in the city
MAY 1907

Chaffinches in the heart of Manchester are certainly unusual, but a correspondent reports that he saw a pair in Queen Street at 9.30 yesterday morning. The hen was sitting on a window ledge, looking dejected, but the cock was lively enough to sing, and then dropped to the ground to feed. My correspondent wonders if the storm of Sunday had driven them from their usual haunts. After all, the birds may not have come any distance, as there are plenty of chaffinches within a short distance of the centre of the city – within the boundaries. I have myself seen larks in the Infirmary yard, and indeed, considering how abundant birds are a short distance from Manchester and how easily they travel, it would be surprising if stragglers did not occasionally wander in.

WTH – I am afraid I cannot tell what the birds seen on Leasowe Links were; the description would apply to many species, and many kinds of birds haunt or pass along the Wirral coast.

HCB – The curious little object picked up on Lytham sandhills is a wind-blown, pebble-rubbed bit of shell – I think a broken-off portion of a whelk shell, with the edges rounded by friction.

Thomas Coward

A plague of grubs
JULY 1907

Delamere Forest has been suffering from a plague of the caterpillars of that little green Tortrix, the oak leaf-roller moth. The foliage of the oaks looks withered and blighted, many branches are stripped of leaves, and the edges of the leaves which remain are neatly rolled-up, having contained in their silk-fastened portions the pupae of the moth. Now the moths are out, swarming everywhere, green and protectively coloured when settled on the foliage, but very conspicuous when on dark bark or flying against a dark background. The damage done by these moths, or rather by their green grubs, is sometimes very serious and this year it is decidedly bad. The entomologist Miss Ormerod said that there was no real remedy for the trouble 'excepting such as may be found in the encouragement of the wild birds', and the birds are certainly doing their best to help us. A pair of blue tits, which were feeding their young in a hole in a tree, were exceedingly busy; every few seconds, one or other of the parents was at the hole with its beak crammed full of the moths; how many hundreds of bodies were packed inside these hungry youngsters it is difficult to estimate. House sparrows have been observed to be 'indefatigable in search' for the grubs, and the friends of this bird will be glad to hear that large numbers are now busily reducing the numbers of the moths also. For once, at any rate, our over-abundant bird is doing some good.

Thomas Coward

Darling buds
JUNE 1908

Mr Beach Thomas in one of his excellent natural history essays declares that the Mayfly seldom appears until June is well in, and that the hawthorn or May is not out usually until the present month. This year both managed to scrape into their proper months by, to use a most unsuitable expression, the skin of their teeth. I found the short-lived Mayfly out in May, but not in its ordinary swarms, and the whitethorn, which is now so beautiful, was out in a few places before the month ended. There is, however, remarkably little of this hedgerow snow compared with some years; but there is yet time, for the buds take long in opening; there may still be a fine show at Whit week. The name of May is attached, somewhat carelessly, to many plants and animals: the whimbrels, for instance, which are called the May-birds, had begun to appear in April, though their biggest migration did not take place until May.

Thomas Coward

Boy and beast
JUNE 1908

The holidays are over and the wild creatures will have an opportunity of settling down to their usual occupations after the disturbances of Whit week. Many birds and beasts have been badly scared by the appearance in their domains of hundreds of Manchester and Salford lads. Most of these lads do not mean to be unkind, but for all that, many animals suffer. One boy, for instance, caught a young rabbit; he wished to own a tame rabbit, and so by way of keeping it safe until his return on Saturday tied it by its back legs to a tree. He innocently told one of his officers about his triumph, and was promptly sent off to release the captive; when he reached the tree, the rabbit had gone. Possibly someone had found it, possibly some bird or beast of prey had released it for its own gain, or, it may be, the rabbit in its struggles had got rid of the cord. We hope this last was the case.

Thomas Coward

Problems with pests
JULY 1909

Round Nantglyn, in the hilly country south-west of Denbigh, holly trees and hedges abound, and this year, I hear from a correspondent, the hedges are everywhere disfigured by brown patches of dead leaves. He has examined the dead branches in many parts of the district, and finds in every case that the bark has been gnawed by some small rodent; on two specimens sent to me these small teeth marks are very distinct. For the last two years rats and mice have been abnormally abundant, the latter causing trouble in the gardens, and my informant thinks that the hollies will be seriously damaged unless something is done to reduce the pests. There are at least three small rodents which may be responsible, and the most likely is the bank vole, which is very fond of holly bark. The wood mouse climbs well, and will eat bark, and in the Nantglyn district I found some years ago that the dormouse, a very local animal, is plentiful. The remedy is a simple and natural one, but may not meet with general approval. I advise my correspondent to tell his gamekeepers, and to get his neighbours to give similar instructions, that no kestrel, owl or weasel shall be destroyed. Possibly the first two are already protected, but it is terribly hard work to convince a gamekeeper that the weasel can do any good. I am sure, however, that the weasel is the very best antidote to a mouse plague.

Thomas Coward

Facts about worms
ᕱᕱ AUGUST 1910 ᕲᕲ

It is rather difficult to answer in one paragraph all the questions about earthworms asked by a Stockport correspondent. Undoubtedly worms travel long distances, but not to avoid being drowned; the fact that they do get drowned is accidental. Leaves are taken down into the holes to be eaten, and not to stop the flow of water; but my correspondent can find full replies and very much more information in Darwin's *Vegetable Mould and Earthworms*.

It is not unusual to see the semi-domestic swan on salt water; probably the cygnets seen at Ayr had not actually been hatched near the sea, but had been led to the water by the old birds.

Thomas Coward

Bad-tempered crabs
SEPTEMBER 1910

Before me, in a jar full of salt water, are some minute hermit crabs and a number of empty shells. The quaint little crustaceans employ themselves in repeated removals; they select a likely shell, handle it with their claws and legs, and then suddenly slip out of the old into their new home. Often, within a minute, they have decided that the new domicile is not as comfortable as the old, and as quickly move back again. When not removing they either devour shreds of meat or fish, for they are bad-tempered little things.

Thomas Coward

Silence and snow
APRIL 1911

Snow was falling this morning when I received news of the arrival in the north of the first chiffchaffs. Two or three were heard in song yesterday afternoon in the woods near Colwyn. I have not heard any so far in Cheshire; on Saturday and Sunday I visited several likely spots, and others were visited by friends, amongst them a locality in the Delamere district where we usually come across this hardy little warbler before March is ended. One can hardly blame it for not hurrying, or, if it is here, for remaining silent.

Thomas Coward

Beauty in the slag

April 1911

Even here in the North, where it has evidently been much milder than in the South of England, the forward trees and shrubs have suffered from the nipping wind and the frost. I hear of the setback at Southport, and the sycamores here are not so flourishing as they were a week ago. On Saturday I was in damson country, and though there were branches laden with buds there was hardly any open blossom visible. Woodland and wayside flowers are scarcer than they should be in the second week of April, with the exception, perhaps of the brave coltsfoot. I found it growing and glowing near Northwich on a chemical spoil-bank, whilst a level stretch of cinders, shunned even by the rankest grass, was dotted with the yellow flowers. Northwich should adopt the coltsfoot as its floral emblem.

Thomas Coward

The Glorious 20th

August 1912

Everyone thinks he knows when grouse may be legally shot, but how many, except sportsmen, are aware that there are four opening days for grouse shooting? Two days before the 12th it was legal to kill the big capercaillie; ptarmigan might be slain on the same day as red grouse; and now on the 20th comes the fatal day for black game, better known as blackcock. In Britain this last bird, though not so locally abundant, has a much wider range than its moorland relative. We might reasonably expect that South-country blackcock would nest earlier than those in sterner, more northerly counties, but, whether they do so or do not, the Somerset, Devon and Hampshire sportsmen are not supposed to shoot them until the season opens for partridges; thus September 1 is the fourth day for grouse. Here in Cheshire, Derbyshire and Staffordshire, where the firwoods extend up the cloughs or border the ling-clad moors, the blackcock and greyhen may be shot tomorrow. On this hilly borderland the bird is still plentiful, but from Delamere, Rudheath and other places where it once occurred in lowland Cheshire – and possibly in south Lancashire – it has vanished, and efforts to reinstate it have failed.

Thomas Coward

The wandering frogs
༽ AUGUST 1912 ༼

We seldom meet the wandering frog or see its crushed corpse on the road; on its nocturnal travels it usually dodges the dangerous wheel or boot. Yet the frog certainly covers considerable distances when seeking fresh feeding grounds. In my own garden there is one small area – very small – reserved for marsh plants, and all summer this spot is guarded by two or three frogs; elsewhere in the garden frogs are mere casuals. There is no water in which tadpoles are reared in the immediate neighbourhood, and it is reasonable to suppose that the place is discovered by chance. The frogs vary in size, and sometimes a new arrival may be recognised. Small, medium-sized and large frogs all seem to wander; the time of travel is not confined to one particular age. Homing instincts of the batrachians have been studied, but this occurrence in a non-breeding but food-supplying spot suggests prospecting rather than homing. The wandering frogs hit on a good place, stake their claims and squat. I hope that they will long continue to squat, for as a pest destroyer few creatures can compete with a healthy frog.

Thomas Coward

A Croydon rarity

SEPTEMBER 1912

An enthusiastic young naturalist, perhaps I may call him a pupil, who has been trapping vigorously, captured an interesting mouse near Croydon. It is an example of the large sub-species which is often called the yellow-necked woodmouse. It is not only longer than the typical wood or long-tailed fieldmouse, but differs from the common species in its marking. The ordinary form often has a spot, small streak or tinge of yellow on the breast and under-surface, but this mouse has a broad band of yellow between the forelegs, and a short extension of yellow forwards towards the neck and backwards from the band; the rest of the underparts are white. So far I have not heard of this large mouse in Lancashire or Cheshire, though I have handled many examples from each county of the typical form.

Thomas Coward

CHAPTER TWO

The Mysterious 'S'

When Thomas Coward was negotiating over the Country Diary in 1904, he specified that he 'did not want to share the column with Nicholson', a name which then disappeared from the paper's correspondence files. But not for ever. When the Coward monopoly was finally broken, it was this Mr Nicholson who took the 15 shillings. He was also from Cheshire but crucially ran a farm there; while Coward concentrated on wildlife and conservation, his new colleague saw things from the potentially conflicting agricultural point of view. The clash of opinions feared by Coward did not arise, however, at least not in print. Perhaps C.P. Scott or his deputies had a word about making room for all views, but there was a more practical reason. Having embarked on varying the daily diaries, Scott had no intention of stopping. There were plenty of possible candidates: John Masefield, for instance, the future Poet Laureate and author of *Reynard the Fox*, who wrote leaders for the *Guardian* and edited Miscellany. But instead, as Europe slid into war, Coward and Nicholson were joined by an enigmatic figure called 'S', who shifted the northern bias of the column by writing from Oxfordshire but gave no other clues to his or her identity. And then a letter from Cross Street arrived on the mat of a prominent, hot-tongued suffragette, Helena Swanwick.

She was the clever child of an unusual couple. Her father Oswald Sickert was a Danish artist who moved to Germany and then Britain in an unsuccessful attempt to make his name. Her mother was the illegitimate daughter of an Irish dancer and a Fellow of Trinity College, Cambridge. To complete the household, she was the sister of Walter Sickert, the artist and friend of Oscar Wilde and Aubrey Beardsley. He has been suggested as Jack the Ripper by the crime writer Patricia Cornwell, whose sources included Helena's reminiscences, *I Have Been Young*. Whatever the likelihood of that, Helena grew up in a bohemian world.

She was also one of the first students at Girton College, Cambridge, where she studied moral sciences before marrying a maths lecturer at Manchester University thirteen years her senior. Strong-minded and independent, she took up politics and journalism in her new home, bearding Scott to give her books to review for the *Guardian* as early as 1899. By 1908 she had won his approval to such an extent that he recommended her to the suffragettes' wealthy backer Frederick Pethick Lawrence as one of only two good women journalists in Britain who supported the cause (as the *Guardian* now did, after an absolute ban while John Edward Taylor was alive). Lawrence needed such advocates; he was imprisoned after using his London house as a hospital for injured activists, and also made to pay for damage caused by the suffragettes' window-smashing campaign.

Helena seems an unlikely writer of the Country Diary, which was to be lampooned during her tenure by Evelyn Waugh's *Scoop*, with its Lush Places column in the *Daily Beast* edited by the unworldly (but ultimately all-conquering) William Boot. In 1914 she was not only editing *Common Cause*, the journal of the National Union of Women's Suffrage Societies, but helping to set up the country's main anti-war movement, the Union of Democratic Control, with the future Labour prime minister Ramsay MacDonald. She advocated premarital sex as women's natural biological response to the prospect of so many men killing one another. But Scott knew that she had also written a short but informative gardening manual, because he had introduced her to its publishers, Sherratt & Hughes. So amid the suffragette turmoil and the slide into world war, he offered her a guinea and a half a week (the equivalent of £130 today) to contribute gardening notes and then, a few months later, Country Diaries.

Mrs Swanwick was to write for the column for the next 25 years, with several periods away when she was overwhelmed with political work, but she seldom mixed her records of plants and animals with social comment. Her 'country' diary was often more of a gardening notebook, with deliberately feminine touches such as worrying over colour clashes in her flower borders at Kew, which were treated as if they were her wardrobe.

Scott continued to look for other voices, especially as rural and wildlife issues rose up the national agenda in spite of the world war, and sometimes because of it. The catastrophe provided unusual material. There were dispatches from the Western Front, where some of the most pitiful records are the lists of birds, flowers and insects on the battlefield compiled by knowledgeable young men, many of whom never came home. Major Arnold Boyd, who supplied Coward with data before succeeding him as diarist, recorded how 'swallows' nests were in some cases signed-for along with other trench stores by relieving troops'. At home, there were similar natural history side effects of the fighting, such as the suggestion that nightingales sang more loudly during Zeppelin raids because they thought the noise of the bombing was made by rival birds. But it was the wider context in the countryside which specially exercised the *Guardian*.

Helena Swanwick: suffragette, peace campaigner and scourge of fruit-tree pests

By 1915 the unexpected scale of mobilisation led to the suspension of the Education Acts in 20 rural counties, so that school-age children could replace farm labourers who had joined the forces. The newspaper campaigned against such measures, comparing the practice to the press gang. In the words of an article by J.L. Hammond whose anger can still be felt, it was 'treason against society'. The establishment of the Agricultural Wages Board in 1917 saw victory in this struggle, a year before the fighting ended in France.

It was perhaps the most important moment of the decade for the countryside. But close behind came a meeting in London in 1912 chaired by Charles Rothschild, father of the redoubtable naturalist Miriam, which set up the Society for the Promotion of Nature Reserves. This became the Royal Society for Nature Conservation and was the parent of the process which now protects so much of the country as national and local nature reserves and sites of special scientific interest. It was very much to the liking of Thomas Coward and his colleagues, whose diaries, modest as they were in terms of space, played a part in convincing the influential that this was not a side issue.

Scott's final new recruit reflected his interest in covering these issues in the Country Diary. He offered weekly space to a professional newsman, R.C. Spencer, who had just retired as the *Guardian*'s chief reporter and moved to London. Spencer had been a loyal foot soldier since 1889, when he was recruited on the strength of a series of nature articles about the Isle of Wight. He survived a rocky period from 1893 to 1895 as editor of the *New Weekly*, Scott's doomed attempt at a 'popular working class weekly' which never recovered from printing pictures upside down in its first issue. Spencer, however, flourished as the *Guardian*'s first real labour correspondent, which gave him useful links with Mrs Swanwick once they were in harness together as Country Diarists. As well as comparing gardening notes, he in Streatham (from which he made forays to study farming in the Home Counties), she in Kew, he knew most of her radical political allies.

And then there was the mysterious 'S', working away anonymously until 1915, when a letter from him arrived on Scott's desk. It is clearly in answer to a query from the editor about the need for such complete disguise, although Scott's letter has not survived. The writer was Basil de Selincourt, a well-known literary and art critic at the time, who had written books on Giotto, William Blake and Walt Whitman. He told Scott that he had opted for the single, unidentifiable letter because 'it seemed in these days – or might seem – a little trivial to be watching insects or enjoying the countryside'.

He went on to make a fundamental assertion of the column's importance which has held good. 'The truth, I am sure, is that relief and reminders of what is normal and sweet in life are more than ever necessary, and I shall waive all scruples in deference to your kind appreciation.' And so 'S' became 'B de S'.

Change at last – in the country and the diarist
OCTOBER 1913

There were signs of coming change on Saturday, but the temperature was still high, flies were numerous, and a few pied wagtails were busy on the lawn in the morning. Probably these birds passed on southward, as we have seen no more of them. On Sunday the air was much colder, and the leaves were falling in showers from the sycamores, limes, elms and birches. The break in the weather seems to have come, and we know well that a frost and a little rough weather will in a single night produce a marvellous change in the landscape. At the moment the oaks and many ash trees are in full leaf and are scarcely changed in colour. Our dahlias, hollyhocks and chrysanthemums are in perfect bloom, and roses are still a wonderful show.

It will interest Manchester citizens and others to know that rain fell heavily in Cumberland on Saturday, as it did also in many other places, and there need now be no fear about our water supply. The 'floating island' in Derwentwater, the occasional appearance of which has been of interest to many scientific people during the past century, came to the surface for a short time, in early September. This curious phenomenon occurs only, as far as I can ascertain, when unusually droughty weather causes the waters of the lake to fall much below the ordinary level, and certain conditions are set up that lead to the rising of this mass of weeds and mud.

A. Nicholson

Puzzling out plants
❧ OCTOBER 1913 ☙

Two plants have been forwarded, and in each case I had to seek expert help before I could name them. The large weed, which was 3ft 6ins high, sent by my Llandudno correspondent, is an amaranth, probably *Amaranthus retroflexus*. It is a 'common warm country European and Asiatic weed' which occasionally is introduced with imported seed and appears as a casual. It has been noticed in both Lancashire and Cheshire near canals and docks, happy hunting grounds for alien plants. This particular specimen was found in a field.

The other plant is a little white upright fungus which was found growing in clumps about three inches in diameter amongst the grass in a meadow near the Trent at Nottingham. It is *Clavaria tenerrima*, and some of the branched fungi of the same genus are commonly known as stag's-horn fungus. I tasted a morsel and found it pleasant; on the Continent several of the family are eaten, but the kinds which grow in England are too small to be worth the trouble of collecting for food. A few days ago I was pleased to find a very beautiful little scarlet club-shaped fungus in my own garden; it is *Torrubia militaris*, which grows above the corpses of caterpillars which have entered the ground in order to pupate; the famous 'vegetable caterpillar' of New Zealand is one of the family. According to most authorities this fungus grows from the pupa, but I have usually found that it has destroyed the caterpillar and turned it into a living fungus.

Thomas Coward

Wet weather
❧ OCTOBER 1913 ☙

Few parts of this country have now to complain of their water supply. Heavy showers have been general, but still the temperature, at least in this neighbourhood, has been high, and our gardens are gay with flowers. Even in the city midges are again flying this morning, though I hope it may be many years before we have such a visitation as we had on Friday last.

Riding through Cheshire today, I found most of the foliage of the woodlands green and perfect, for many of the trees are oaks and ashes, and the grass, which is still growing, is fresh and green. Some will say that there is not much feeding quality in this autumn growth, but the cattle like it, it keeps them healthy, and farmers well know it saves the provender. To the dairy farmer it is a great help as it keeps his herd in good milking condition, and with the troubles he has to face now, owing to higher railway rates and the difficulty he has to contend with in raising his price for milk, this fine, open autumn weather is very welcome. The shepherd too has great gain from this abundant herbage for his ewes, just at the time he is wanting to bring them to a condition of perfect health, and all his flock will greatly benefit by having good food in plenty. Again this morning, as I passed certain fields, I found the band of brown earth from which the potatoes had been cleared broader, and another stubble ploughed. The outdoor work of the farm is well forward.

A. Nicholson

On the eve of Armageddon
ॐ AUGUST 1914 ॐ

The drenching showers of rain this weekend have been most unfortunate for the holidays. I cannot say that I think the garden has suffered, but it is bad for the farmer. With labour so insufficient it is difficult to see how he is to get the necessary work done in the turnip fields and elsewhere, and win the harvest which, when opportunity offers, must be his first object.

The high temperature and ample rainfall, producing quite 'forcing weather', has entirely changed the appearance of our orchard. Some sorts of apples are full size, or near it, and pears and plums have filled out quickly. Of morello cherries, which are now ripening, there has been a very good crop this season.

A. Nicholson

Wildlife and war
ᴥ MAY 1915 ᴧ

The question how far the changes in the habits of men this year will affect those of animals and birds naturally presents itself. Our disposition probably is to exaggerate the amount of disturbance likely to be caused. Migrating birds would no doubt avoid a battle, but they would flit over entrenched lines or even along them, were that necessary, unnoticing and unnoticed. Birds accustomed to human habitation do not need buildings in good repair and ruined villages will house swifts, swallows and martins as happily as if nothing were amiss. Shyer varieties will often find their haunts pre-occupied, but in compensation the countryside in general will be quieter; there seems little reason to suppose that many French or Belgian birds will come as far as England. In this country disturbance will occur chiefly in the neighbourhood of army camps; the inhabitants of downs and commons and those that nest in the furze will be aware of unusual bustle in their familiar haunts, even when their breeding sites have not been cleared away to make room for tents or huts. Thus a good many will have to put up with conditions or localities they prefer to avoid. The stonechat has already been seen twice in this part of Oxfordshire, though we have little land suitable for it and it has only once been recorded as breeding here. We shall look out also for the wheatear, a bird confined as a rule to our higher slopes, and even then seen only occasionally.

I must thank 'Oxoniensis' for his note on the cuckoo. From him I learn that north-east Oxon heard it three days before north-west — i.e. as early as Saturday, 24 April.

Basil de Selincourt

A palace underground
SEPTEMBER 1915

I have been digging out a wasps' nest which had been made in a heap of turves in my Oxfordshire garden, and believe it to be an unusually large one. The construction was interesting, the nest itself not being opposite the hole by which the wasps entered to it, but tucked away at the end of a passage of appreciable length on the left. It consisted of ten tiers of circular combs, of which the middle comb was of course the largest, and was about twice the size of an Association football. I counted the cells in the largest of these combs and estimated that there were some 150 in the outermost ring alone and close upon 50 along the diameter. The whole comb must therefore have accommodated 2,000 grubs at least, and the nest have been capable of rearing anything from ten to twenty thousand wasps at a time. The cavity left in the turf heap after I had removed it was a very curious sight, and suggested the interior view of the dome of a church; but of course the floor was dome-like as well as the roof. An immense quantity of fine earth must have been carried away by the workers in the course of construction, but they were not able to dispose of stones, so their habitation rested on a good pile of pebbles of various sizes. This was no doubt an accidental feature, but in the event of heavy rains might have been of great service as drainage to the nest.

Basil de Selincourt

Drilling in the dark
❧ NOVEMBER 1915 ☙

The cold storms of the last few days were heralded here by a party of seagulls that flew overhead in leisurely circles from the eastward last Sunday, making, no doubt, for the more protected beaches of the Bristol Channel. In spite of inclement weather, a thrush has continued valiantly singing in a neighbour's shrubbery, and I have little doubt that the warm weather last month tempted him to a belief in spring and that his mate has eggs somewhere. There is nothing very uncommon in a thrush's nest in October, but from the grounds of the same neighbour a much rarer event is recorded, viz., autumn building by a pair of rooks. Yesterday's chilly and drenching rains must have been a severe discouragement to these untimely breeders.

The storm here has a curious magnetic or electric quality. Although the sky was hidden last night by scarcely broken clouds, and there was, of course, no moon, it was light enough at nine in the evening for our local volunteer recruits to drill without losing their formation. We could quite make out one another's faces at five yards.

Basil de Selincourt

Away from the war
❧ DECEMBER 1915 ☙

In Kew Gardens they leave the Siberian crabs unharvested, and this year the crop has been of a magnificence never surpassed. Several weeks ago, every leaf had fallen, but the thousands of shining fruits still hang on and light up with the sun, the trees from a distance looking as if they were on fire. It is a singular effect and most beautiful. For the most part the colours in a winter garden are quieter than this, but they are infinitely varied if planting has been intelligently done. Berries, evergreens, the varieties of tint in bark and wood, and the remainder of dried-up reeds and grasses and bamboos make up the chief sources of colour, but there is no season when flowers are not to be had, too. One of the things one appreciates in the country after so long sojourning in town is the exquisite variety of shades in the stems of trees and shrubs. In towns even healthy trees are of a uniform black. In a country garden or plantation each kind has its distinct shade of colour. The arbutus is in every way one of the most beautiful of the smaller trees, and its bark is one of its chief beauties. This is of a warm Indian red, and the tint runs to the tips of the smallest twigs, threading the glossy deep green leaves with colour throughout. As the bark grows older, it peels off in a thin papery curl, leaving a most delicious pale green stem revealed. *Arbutus andrachne* is even more beautiful in this way than the commoner *Arbutus unedo*, and there is a fine hybrid between the two. The shape of this romantic tree is as beautiful as its stem and leaf, and the pretty heath-like white flower is followed by crimson bells about the size of a small cherry, and very persistent.

Helena Swanwick

A soldier misbehaves
MAY 1916

I learn from a Southport correspondent that a few days ago a crack shot in the National Reserve shot a pair of dotterel out of a group of seven on the shore between Southport and Preston. Parties or 'trips' of dotterel still pass on migration along our Lancashire coast and a few pairs, very few, nest in the Lake District and on some of the Scottish mountains. The bird must not be confused with the ringed plover, often known as the ring dotterel, which nests upon the Lancashire beaches; it is a far rarer bird, and is quite rightly specially protected. But in spite of protection and the fact that it is now the close season, the law is openly defied, and, worse still, by a soldier. What is the use of county council orders and where are the police who are, in spite of the war, supposed to see that civil laws are obeyed?

For some strange reason, fly-fishers seem to think that at certain times or in certain places trout (or it may be salmon) will only rise to artificial flies made with dotterel feathers. I do not mind if I am offending the fly-fishing fraternity, and perhaps I am wrong in my ideas about these flies, but I do know that makers of flies use dotterel feathers, and that these two illegally slaughtered birds were given to a man in order that he might pluck their beautiful feathers from them and make them up into a lure for fish! The same gunner brought down a wood pigeon which had in its crop no fewer than 553 grains of barley; there the man was doing good and breaking no law. What a pity that he could not confine his attention to the harmful wood-pigeons which, by the way, are much more difficult to shoot than confiding migrant dotterels!

Thomas Coward

Home front farming
NOVEMBER 1916

A night frost made everything appear in the morning as though it had been covered with a light fall of very fine snow. But when this melted with a slight shift of wind a touch of green came across one of the lower ploughfields. It is not a large stretch of Surrey land – the farmer calls it a 'patch of corn' – harrowed and sown broadcast by hand while the surface was rather soft for a drill. There is always pleasure in the sight of these first shoots; you note their coming from one side just where the faint light of the sun shines about noon, then cross to the other side and wait to see birds fly over from the meadow, where the tops of the grass here and there have withered to a dull brown. A farm hand is lifting Swedes in the turnip field and trimming off the green tops with a bill, packing them in sacks for market. When this old labourer pauses for a rest he chops a root asunder, tosses half to a heifer that has come inquisitively across from the barnyard, cuts off a slice for himself, nibbles, pulls up his sheepskin glove, and sets to work again. The afternoon turns grey and raw, and the wind is mournful in the bare elms. While a few small flakes are tossed in various directions, a missel thrush starts his first song from the extreme branch of a pear tree in the orchard. It is but a few notes at a time with long pauses between, but it enlivens us all just here about the farm.

R.C. *Spencer*

Coward gives Helena a lesson
December 1916

A writer who knows vastly more than I do about birds thinks that my reply about wagtails is misleading, and I hasten to communicate his further notes, to supplement the bird authority whom I quoted recently. 'The pied and grey wagtails', writes my informant, 'are both migrants as well as residents – the majority of each species returning south in autumn. Some individuals remain in the South of England all winter, but others go overseas. A few, but only a few of each remain at or near breeding stations. If you include as species the blue-headed and grey-headed wagtails, you should also include the ashy-headed, black-headed and Sykes's wagtails. The white wagtail has also bred here. The correct description of most of our so-called resident birds is resident and migratory.'

It is clear from this that, if my former correspondent saw water wagtails recently, they would be some of those which have not gone south; but it would be a mistake to suppose that the pied or water wagtails do not migrate; the majority of them do. This point is now made clear in all bird books.

Helena Swanwick

Owls in the trenches

JANUARY 1917

Several correspondents in France have referred to the owls which find the trenches such profitable mouseries that they hunt by day. The latest note on the subject comes from one of our south coast camps where a light brown owl – probably a barn owl – found daylight sport anything but peaceful. The lads who were watching it were not the trouble, but a number of gulls resented its presence 'and flew excitedly round it', though apparently they did not venture to attack the unusual-looking bird. Then a rook, no doubt attracted by the calls of the gulls, came along, flying above the owl. It darted upon the mouse-hunter, striking it on the back with its beak, and down fell the owl. 'We saw it no more,' writes my correspondent, but it does not follow that the owl was slain; a rook coming down with wings half-closed, 'stooping' like a falcon, is certainly a formidable foe, but the feathers on an owl's back are wonderfully thick and soft and would act as an elastic cushion, protecting the body.

A small bird which 'seems to fly in jumps' has puzzled the same correspondent; it is black and white with a 'black boomerang band on its white throat' and white streaks – outer feathers – on the tail. Undoubtedly our friend the pied wagtail; many of these birds are now wintering on our southern shores.

Thomas Coward

Back from the Front
❧ NOVEMBER 1918 ❧

The steady rise in the barometer we hope indicates a continuance of the fine weather, for though it is accompanied by a fall in the temperature light frosts will aid the ploughman, and it is his great autumn work about which we are anxiously thinking. Though we have at last a cessation of hostilities, there is in all European countries such a shortage of food that we must make every possible endeavour to grow food in our own country. The success we have had in the past twelve months ought to be a great incentive. Although the weather during the past two months has held us back, we may expect to have more help in the coming time and be able to work and plant more ground than for many past seasons. Some of the first to return from service will be the young farmers, and many who have been working at munitions and other war work will be able to return to the land.

A. Nicholson

Town and country
❧ NOVEMBER 1918 ❧

Many parts of these islands would be troublesome to classify if one allowed only the two divisions of town and country. There are miles upon miles in Durham and in Derbyshire and South Wales and here in Lanarkshire which certainly are not town miles, and almost as certainly not country; at least not 'pure country'. For great heaps of slag rear their unnatural straight lines above the fields and great chimneys belch forth smoke and fire and the streams are polluted. Yet within a few yards of the great works and of the pitheads, ploughing is well on its way and the bloomy furrows lie with the frost daintily picking them out.

By and by the rolling land breaks into a deep clough, wooded with birch, very sombre in the bare branches, chalky white in the stems, which gleam ghostly in the waning light. When we have climbed the farther bank and walked across a few more fields, curiously painted with kale in tartan pattern, we get out of the roar of the stream and into a very still desolation. The grass is already its winter dust colour and slopes on all sides to the bare edges of a little lake. The thin ice is just strong enough for one silent gull to alight upon it. The moon is nearly full in the frosty sky, and not far off we can see the intermittent blaze of the ironworks.

The people reflect the strange mixture. They live with an intensity of local communal feeling unlike the isolation of the country, but still more unlike the blunted herd-instinct of the town.

Helena Swanwick

Spinning out rations
ꙅ DECEMBER 1918 ꙅ

The extensive use of 'kindle-wood' and other timber to make our fuel rations spin out may, as a side-issue, influence the number of insects and other invertebrates next season. Old and fallen branches and trunks with loose bark, especially when slightly rotten, are the winter refuges of an immense number of small animals; we not only destroy their shelters but cremate the sleeping victims. Much of this latent life is in the egg stage, but many insects hibernate as larvae, pupae, and in their final, perfect state; beetles burrow into the wood itself or mine the timber beneath the bark; woodlice and spiders, centipedes and millipedes, slugs, and even worms hide in cracks and crannies. Some of these are our foes but many are our friends, and all alike perish in the flames.

When cutting up a block of oak, I came across a dense knot of earthworms, flaccid and lethargic; they had found a spot where the damp had entered and rotted the hard tissues. I turned them out and a robin came to investigate but did not seem to care too much about them; a blackbird or thrush would have provided decent interment for the lot. It seems a pity to destroy useful creatures like spiders, worms and carnivorous beetles but, after all, what is useful and what harmful? The predacious animal does not care about economic values; it devours other carnivorous creatures as well as those we think are our enemies because they feed on plants. Some of our worst pests destroy weeds as well as edible vegetables. The ways of nature are apt to be complicated.

Thomas Coward

Fear of flying
JANUARY 1919

We have grown so familiar with the aeroplane that its boom passes almost unnoticed; we do not, perhaps, trouble to cross a road to obtain a better view of the machine, whereas a few years ago everyone stopped and gazed skywards immediately the sound caught the air. It is exactly the same with birds. A few years ago, the appearance of an aeroplane caused great consternation among these lesser flyers; rooks, pigeons, starlings, partridges and others scattered and took cover, long before our less keen eyes had spotted the approaching machine. Now they are indifferent. The noise of engines caused me to look up and I saw a long flight of gulls and lapwings passing northeast, following the line of the Ship Canal and probably heading for the flooded meadows. Then, at a fair altitude above them, I saw an aeroplane travelling westwards, but even when it was directly over them, not a bird swerved from its steady course or appeared to notice the strange 'fowl' overhead. Presumably they had learned that this stiff-winged, noisy creature is not a gliding hawk, and that it does not swoop upon or strike down any of their kind. But does

each bird learn this lesson in its youth, or is there an acquired hereditary knowledge? I leave this problem to the avian psychologist, for
it is beyond me.

Thomas Coward

Chemical warfare
❧ FEBRUARY 1919 ❧

I am always glad when I have safely finished the washing of the fruit
trees with caustic soda; it is such dangerous stuff. When measuring
out the powder (1lb to four gallons of water) one's eyes and throat
smart, and later, when spraying with a fine nozzle, one has to be
careful not to get the wrong side of the wind. I chose what seemed
a perfectly still day, but the very fine spray was sensitive to tiresome
little veering gusts, and I was glad I was wearing glasses and gloves.
But what satisfaction to see the result! I had just put in some young
fruit trees, well grown and likely, but decidedly dirty with moss.
Now the moss is entirely destroyed, and in time this batch of trees
will have bark as bright and clean as those which have been cared for
every year in the little plot.

It was a pleasure to do the planting. Dwarf pyramids, close
pruned, are best for a tiny patch. The holes are dug deep enough just
to cover the topmost roots and wide enough to spread all the roots
thoroughly. We do not loosen the soil below, because we want to dis-
courage tap-roots; but we fill in with good, fine soil, rubbing it well
among the roots by hand, and only treading in when we have a good
layer of soil superposed. This soil is very poor and hungry sand, so
after a year's treatment with well-rotted refuse and lime we have
added a little basic slag when planting, and we have given a mulch of
well-rotted stable manure.

Helena Swanwick

CHAPTER THREE

North and South

One of the most welcome visitors to the *Guardian*'s Cross Street offices during the 1920s was a man with a bald dome of a head, round specs and a droopy moustache who was caricatured by one of the office artists with four swift strokes of an inkbrush. This was Arthur Ransome, later to become famous for his Swallows and Amazons children's books, but at the time a celebrated foreign correspondent for the paper. He had married Trotsky's mistress, an unbeatable way of getting scoops for a journalist in early Soviet Russia. One of his other ploys was to impress junior Communist officials into opening doors by flourishing a crested letter from the London Library demanding the return of overdue books. He was given a long series of special commissions which were taken very seriously by all concerned. When he went to Shanghai in 1927 and arrived half-dead from flu after crossing Siberia by train, his instructions to be left alone in bed to recover were flouted, as he reported, by 'contacts in both Chinese and European dress who batter at my door from nine in the morning until after midnight. All sides seem equally impressed with getting the truth to the *Manchester Guardian*.'

For all the glamour of this overseas work, Ransome received more readers' letters about another side to his journalism: his natural history and countryside pieces in the *Guardian*, which later coloured the landscape in which his young heroes did battle in their dinghies. It was largely for the outstanding descriptions of the natural world that his book *Pigeon Post* won the first Carnegie Medal, for an outstanding children's book, in 1936. He turned out columns on everything from The Joys of Motoring in the North of England to Rod and Line, an angling feature which had an enormous following. A typical example taken at random and published on 4 September 1925, next to an exciting item about a Turkish pasha escaping from a Sussex mental home, starts: 'There was just the beginning of light in the sky and the thick mist over river and meadow was already white . . .' And so we are off, bewitched.

Ransome never wrote a Country Diary but he was an influential adviser and headhunter for C.P. Scott when it came to finding fresh candidates for the job. He lived in an isolated cottage at Ludderburn in the Lake District (with no telephone, which infuriated the foreign newsdesk), and much admired the first diarist to be based in that part of England, George W. Muller. A German immigrant who was considered the best fly-fisher in the north of England, Muller was an expert rock-climber, one of the great gossips of Westmorland and very knowledgeable about hunting. In Ransome's words: 'He knows the otter more intimately than most men know their own cats.'

More than almost any other Country Diarist, Muller felt the wrath of *Guardian* readers because of his interest in hunting. A regular column which he was given to write about the subject, alongside the diary, was scrapped after an organised campaign. He took the field sportsman's view that hunting was a responsible way of controlling wild animal populations, especially when carried out by

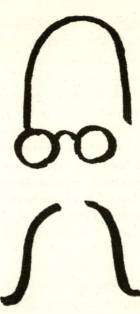

**MR. ARTHUR RANSOME TAKES ADVANTAGE
OF THIS YEAR'S EXTRA DAY TO VISIT
MANCHESTER.**

*Ransome was usually out and about as a roving 'fireman' journalist.
This cartoon marks a rare leap-year appearance in the office*

people who knew more about the fox, stag or otter than many of
their detractors. The principle is illustrated in an exchange he had
towards the end of his life with A.P. Wadsworth, editor of the
Guardian from 1944 to 1956, who had sent him an excessively bloodthirsty book about otter-hunting. Muller returned it from his home
in Cockermouth with a note saying: 'I am sure you would not wish
me to review a book in which so much delight is taken in killing.'
Death was not the point for him; he added: 'Perhaps you may not

remember the outcry of the Society of Friends to Mr Scott against my hunting stories, in which blood was never hinted at. I mourn the loss of the weekly guinea, and now and again I remind my Quaker friends how they did me down.'

Muller could not placate the anti-bloodsports partisans but he had a sure touch with fellow naturalists and, like Coward, used a network to help him cover his beat. After Ransome's Rod and Line was dropped in 1929, Muller campaigned for its return, writing to Cross Street to say: 'I know at least 30 MG readers in Cumberland who would welcome 2–300 words on angling in Cumbrian waters.' This sure grasp of an area was in tune with natural history developments at the time. In 1926 the Norfolk Naturalists' Trust was established, the first of a county-based network which gradually expanded to cover virtually the whole of the country.

Muller's deployment in the Lakes reinforced the northern side of the Country Diary, while Helena Swanwick, R.C. Spencer and Basil de Selincourt dealt with the south – although, then as now, this tended to mean London or nearby. In 1924 the chance arose for a wider spread when Mrs Swanwick was offered the editorship of *Foreign Affairs*, the journal of the Union of Democratic Control, and asked Scott if she could take a break. In the same letter she started a practice which was to become the norm when a diarist retired, by effectively nominating her successor. 'I suppose you hadn't thought of Will Arnold Foster?' she wrote. 'He lives near the Land's End and is the owner and chief gardener of a most uncommon garden of boulders and Himalayan shrubs. An astonishing person because he is also the keenest painter and an expert in foreign affairs.'

As in later successions, at least one of which was actually hereditary, Mrs Swanwick was anointing a friend and ally. Arnold Foster was a barrister who supported disarmament. He went to Geneva on behalf of pacifist groups and was used by Ramsay MacDonald's Labour government as a special adviser. He had to stop his Country Diary in 1930 when he was appointed a temporary civil servant with the Privy Council. In a letter to Scott on the council's grandly embossed notepaper, he described himself as 'muzzled', although he was back in touch before the end of the year with the news that he had resigned so that 'I can feel free to write and speak again.'

Arnold Foster lived on the Cornish cliffs in a house called Eagle's Nest and was a vigorous campaigner for the West Country's wild places. When he was appointed at Christmas 1924, he modestly deferred to George Muller, telling Scott, 'I have an average knowledge of the birds and beasts though nothing like your Cumberland correspondent's.' But he cited an interest in the peregrines, seals, herons and badgers which were still abundant in Cornwall but threatened by new farming practices, hunting and pollution. He was delighted that the last mammal to be discovered in Britain – the Scilly shrew – was classified in the year of his appointment as a diarist.

He also had a uniquely intimate take on the Country Diary practice of relying on others. While Coward and Muller used reports from fellow field naturalists, Arnold Foster turned to his wife. When he gave up the Country Diary after leaving Cornwall for the Privy Council, he wrote to Scott: 'I have now moved to London and my wife – who has been doing the notes for me for several weeks – is coming to London too.' This accounts for the brief replacement of the initials WAF with KAF, which those familiar with the *Guardian*'s reputation for misprints might have dismissed as a gremlin. It also gave the paper probably its most exotic Country Diary writer: Katherine Arnold Foster was better known as Ka Cox, the name she used before her marriage. The striking bohemian friend of Virginia Woolf and D.H. Lawrence and mother of a stillborn child by her fellow Neo-Pagan the poet Rupert Brooke, she died in memorable circumstances in 1938, after a confrontation with the self-styled 'Great Beast' Aleister Crowley over some supposedly satanic rituals at a cottage on the moor where the badgers in her diary, below, had their sett.

The final recruit in this raffish period of the diary's history was another character from the fringe of Bloomsbury, the classical scholar Janet Case, who had appeared in 1883 in the all-male Cambridge University's triennial Greek play – a production which later saw the *Times* critic enraptured by the 'exceedingly beautiful' Rupert Brooke. No other woman was to join the cast until the future Baroness Brigstocke in 1950. Miss Case, who lived with her sister Emma in the New Forest, taught Greek to the teenage Virginia Woolf and although the writer's memoirs are unreliable, she left a memorable vignette of revealing to her teacher that her stepbrother George Duckworth was sexually abusing her. 'To my surprise she [Janet Case] has always had an intense dislike of him; and used to say "Whew, you nasty creature," when he came in and began fondling me over my Greek. When I got to the bedroom scenes, she dropped her lace, and gaped like a benevolent gudgeon. By bedtime she was feeling quite sick.'

Darling buds of February
❧ FEBRUARY 1920 ❧

It is many years since vegetation was so advanced at this season as it is this year. A wail comes to me from a Herefordshire garden where the flower-buds are appearing on the roses. Crocuses are fully out and the elms are reddening with myriads of flowers.

I amused myself this week by making a doll's garden for a sick friend, and in the moss-filled bowl there were *Iris reticulata*, the proud purple queen over all; *Iris danfordiae*, golden and green; *Cyclamen coum*, crimson; a white crocus, violets, arabis, snowdrop, winter aconite, periwinkle, polyanthus, primrose, Siberian squill, a spray of *Lithospermum* with gentian-blue flower, and one or two tufts of sweetbriar and leaves of balm and bergamot. If larger flowers had been permissible, there would have been a fine show of hellebores.

Helena Swanwick

Pointless killing

᎒᎒ MARCH 1920 ᎒᎒

Anything that gives the destroyer of useful birds an excuse for shooting should be avoided, but at the same time those who wish to
protect birds defeat their own purpose by blinding themselves and
others by their statements about the habits of certain predatory
species. I am fully convinced that the kestrel is a valuable ally of the
farmer, and that the damage it does to young game is far outweighed
by its usefulness in destroying small mammalian pests; nevertheless
it is foolish to say that it never kills birds or that it only eats rats, mice
and beetles. Anyone who knows at once realises that such statements are erroneous, and therefore detract from the value of any
argument in favour of the bird.

The other day I was shown a young female kestrel which had
been shot just after it knocked over a lapwing. My friend who shot
the bird would not believe that a kestrel would dare to attack so large
and unusually plucky a bird as our familiar peewit. The explanation
appears to me simple; there is great individuality among birds. We
meet with criminals and desperadoes amongst peaceful and law-
abiding citizens; we need not expect that every kestrel abides by all
the rules and regulations of its society. The bird was an exception,
but there are no rules without exceptions.

Thomas Coward

Clashing colours

᎒᎒ MAY 1921 ᎒᎒

Among the reconcilers of warring colours I find the meadow rues
most satisfactory. *Thalictrum dipterocarpum*, one of the loveliest of
fairies, I have found difficult, but the meadow rue with the
columbine leaf (*T. aquilegifolium*) is the easiest pretty thing, and lasts

a long time in beauty. Its habit is charming, and its inflorescence, creamy or pink or purple, blends well with all sorts of sharper colours and harmonises them. *T. glaucum*, which is very much taller, has a leaf almost as blue-green as the carnation, and when the fluffy maize-coloured flowers are out it makes a good background for purple salvia or Belladonna larkspur.

Helena Swanwick

Incredible journey
❧ JUNE 1921 ☙

There is nothing surely much more wonderful or interesting than the migration from the sea of the elvers and their ascent of a river and their distribution over the whole of its watershed. We watched the young eels, a little longer and a little thicker than a darning needle, writhing their way over the concrete bed of a mill lade. The water was six inches deep and ran strongly. One and all disappeared down a crack in the concrete four feet away from the quiet water above so nearly won. Some emerged again to be swept down a yard or two, but these struggled back to the crack to dive for a secret and an easier way lakewards.

We spent much time trying to locate the outlet. We discovered it at last in the chamber within which the mill wheel revolves. The sluice was down and the wheel at rest. On this side of the wall dividing the wheel from the overflow lade was a thin trickle of water. It came from the fissure in the concrete. The elvers issued there from and dropped into a pool at the base of the wheel. After that they wriggled up the damp scoop to the sluicegate bottom. Many of them were climbing up the walls. The number of elvers this summer is exceptionally large.

Clinging to the wet moss we found scores of young lampreys, easily recognisable by their gill slits, the number of which gives the lamprey the name we knew it by when we were boys — 'seven holes'.

George Muller

Fungal foray
SEPTEMBER 1922

The long dry summer with its occasional hot days has been favourable to the mysterious subterranean growth which precedes the appearance of mushrooms, and the autumn rains are becoming known at just the right time. Why mushrooms grow sometimes in one field and sometimes in another I have never heard explained, nor whether the conscientious removal of every aspirant discourages the plant. The delights of mushroom-gathering in our district are almost wholly imaginary. I walk the fields dreaming of an exquisite constellation of fairy foot-stools which will be visible on the smooth-shaven green a quarter of a mile away (I did once see such a thing on the cliffs in Cornwall). I occasionally perceive lurking in a tuft of grass a half-grown, twisted specimen, with difficulty freeing itself from the withered bents, of which four or five are embedded in the flesh. But I pick it thankfully, and if I am lucky enough to find a dozen they wonderfully enrich the morning bacon.

Basil de Selincourt

Trouble with tits 1
MARCH 1923

The tits began it. I think there can be no doubt about that. They began it, but the sparrows soon learned the new devilry from them and bettered their instructions. They stand on the branches of the dwarf pear tree and tweak off the flower buds, just as these begin to part from the sheath, and they strew the ground with them. If you watch them (and it is hard to do this with patience) you are amazed at their speed and dexterity. The sparrows do it with a spiteful flick. The tits are more adept at hanging on by their eyelids where the sparrows dare not venture and also at burrowing into the less open buds. Between them, they destroyed all hope even of blossom on two Cadillacs, a Jargonelle and a Beurre d'Amanlie. I sprayed the later trees not yet attacked with Paris green, in the hope that it might prove distasteful. Their friend who fed them through the winter looks reproachfully at them and says: 'Who'd have thought it of you?' – and then wistfully, 'Do you think if I gave them more fat than I do it would keep them away?' I don't. But what is one to do? I find it impracticable to net any but wall fruit.

Helena Swanwick

The hangman's gibbet
⟡ AUGUST 1924 ⟡

An unpleasant odour came from a glade in the big planting where pheasants, most of them immature birds, were feeding. We were not inclined to tarry, but the sight of rabbits hung up on a pole excited our curiosity and we examined them. And we realised almost immediately that an odour of the decomposing flesh was one that would be sniffed by the pheasants in the gamekeeper's care. This was his dodge for keeping his charges from straying. For the rabbit flesh was 'fly blown', and on the ground were the gentles dropping to form a feast greatly esteemed by game birds. There is occasional trouble, of course, with foxes, carrion crows and magpies, all attracted by any kind of beastliness, but vermin soon learns the danger of frequenting a zone where it may itself be gibbeted. Higher up the fell, among the bracken, we came upon a fowl that had been recently devoured by a fox. The fell foxes are extraordinarily numerous this year, and they are raiding the poultry runs around the farmsteads at noonday.

George Muller

Then as now
❦ MAY 2003 ❧

I stumbled upon them by accident and found them both shocking and mesmerising, like all powerful statements of death. Two foxes had been strung up from a hazel bush and the freshest of the skins had all the attributes of the beast: that beautiful rusty tone of fur, the luxurious brush dangling down over its back, the acutely angled snout and head. The other had obviously been swinging throughout the spring and was a mere husk of ribs, blackened bone and grinding teeth, like the negative image for the photograph dangling by its side.

I was reminded of walking through the western highland forests of Cameroon several years ago. My guide Moses and I would come upon assembled wood piles draped with a loop of knotted grasses and Moses would explain that they were full of dangerous power. Any man who tried to steal the wood and disturb the fetish would suffer terrible consequences, such as his penis dropping off.

Stringing up foxes suggests to me that the same ancient responses to life still survive in the English countryside. If anything the fox gibbet is even more primitive. At least the grass fetish has a perfectly understandable rationale, but stringing up your enemies by their feet seems a strange brute exclamation, a summoning down of dark magic. I should add that I have no real problem with control of foxes. They can be as much a problem for environmental organisations as they are for keepers of pheasants or the neighbour with chickens. But the magical ritual surrounding their carcasses was disturbing.

Mark Cocker

The wonder of waste
❧ DECEMBER 1925 ☙

Innocently as well as intentionally man destroys birds and other animals; he drives them away by the spread of cultivation as well as by the growth of residential areas. But, also unconsciously, he supplies them with food and saves them in times of stress. What man does not want he throws away, but birds and animals see that it is not wasted. How they bless the thaw, these children of the open! Old cabbage leaves, turnip tops, potato haulms are no longer fast bound to the iron-hard earth; they can be dragged aside by the plovers, rooks, larks and finches. Sleepy insects shelter beneath them; the worms have pushed up through the softening soil to drag down rotting scraps; wasted grain and other seeds have been safely covered during the frost. Now that the sparkling crystals, which decorated but concealed, have vanished, there are indications how life was supported during the frost, for wherever roots – swedes, turnips, beets or potatoes – lie unearthed in the fields or have been thrown aside as useless, they show great wounds where rabbits, rats and mice have nibbled or rooks and daws hacked with their powerful beaks. And the municipal rubbish heap, a harbour of refuge during the strenuous days, is still frequented by a busy, hungry crowd of starlings, rooks, daws, sparrows and chaffinches, black-headed gulls and one or two winter-soiled pied wagtails which elected to remain behind when their brethren migrated. Birds, at any rate, do not look with favour on destructors.

Thomas Coward

Swing of the scythe
❧ JULY 1926 ☙

Our hay is almost the last to be cut and cleared. The grass was already ripe and parched to brownness before the weather broke, and its feathery flowers made shifting waves of pink and purple at the top. But the big employer who works a large farm gets the start and whips in all available labour. His hay is cut with a machine, horse-drawn. Round after round it goes in narrowing circles in one field after another. The rest of us cut it by hand, and one never grows tired of watching that rhythmic swing of the body as the scythe is drawn back and then swept through an arc with the swish of cut stalks, while the grass falls over and lies in its track, swathe after swathe. Our turn has come at last. The hay has been cut and tossed and heaped in cocks, and now it is being loaded on the cart while helping hands glean the straw wisps with the wide wooden rake. They are racing a storm that threatens. A few drops fall. But the last load is just carried and the field left bare before the rain comes, streaming, soaking down.

Janet Case

Unromantic harvest
SEPTEMBER 1927

They are up in the apple trees harvesting. A man turns on the ladder, among the boughs, releasing with a magnificent gesture a torrent of greens and crimsons. Here's the tree of Cornish Gillyflowers, pale yellow, almost white. And here's a washing basket brimful of Bloody Warriors, so deeply crimson that even the inside of the bitten one is crimson-dyed.

Why is it that the pears' names are mostly French and the apples' names mostly English? Doyenne de Comice, Beurre d'Amanlie, Marguerite Marillat, Marie Louise – I mustn't forget plain English Williams. But all England is storied in the apple names: Peasgood Nonesuch, Ribston Pippin, Quarrendon, Worcester Pearmain, even in the quite modern ones such as William Crump – good, plain English Crump.

But I wish our Northerners made more of a song about harvesting apples. Those Southerners, heaping up oranges and lemons in the groves of the Golden Horn of Palermo, or the family all turned out for the olive-gathering in Tuscany – Ettore, Dario, Marietta, all the lot of them singing; they give the miracle a more cheery welcome than the gardener and his boy can contrive with us.

Will Arnold Foster

Elusive earwigs
NOVEMBER 1928

A touch of frost, sufficient to make the lawn too hard to be tapped or probed for worms, sent the blackbirds and thrushes to the berry-bearing trees and shrubs. But the starlings were clinging like tits to an old brick wall, their claws fast in the bleached masses of wandering sailor, and picking off the insects and grubs that the plant harbours. I looked with new interest at the festoons of wandering sailor, and found here and there grey slugs that the starlings had not yet gobbled.

In the evening I watched a nurseryman hunting in a greenhouse with a torch for earwigs spoiling his chrysanthemum blossoms. Slugs and caterpillars biting the stems below the buds were in plenty, but these he left to the last as easy prey. 'Cunning creatures, these earwigs,' he said. 'You have to pounce on them, else they'll lick you. They don't try to hide or fly. They simply fall out of danger.' As he spoke, an earwig that had eaten a channel in a flower let go and disappeared. 'There you are,' commented the gardener. 'I shall have to wait another night for that chap.'

George Muller

An early oil slick
ᨓ FEBRUARY 1929 ᨕ

Apparently I missed the account of the accident to a tanker on the Mersey Bar, but the lost oil seems to have drifted about on the tide, and perhaps it is still drifting and has already caused a rise in avian casualties. A friend who watches birds in the Isle of Man tells me that large numbers of razorbills, scoters or black ducks, and a few guillemots, natives of the island, have been washed up. Most of the birds were dead and others were doomed, for once they get the nasty clogging oil on their feathers they can neither fly nor swim quickly enough under water to catch fish. Weakened by starvation, they drift ashore and die. Even such powerful birds as great northern divers suffered, for my friend found two, and a rare visitor, a longtailed duck, was in a sorry state although it still had strength to keep off the rocks. The unfortunate diving birds get into trouble when they come up from a dive if they happen to rise within one of the circles of floating oil. Oil may still troubled water but it troubles diving birds until they are permanently still.

Thomas Coward

A cub's adventure
ᨓ JANUARY 1930 ᨕ

An otter cub squeaked on the other side of the river. The bailiff did not locate it for twenty minutes, and then he had to walk a mile and a half to the opposite bank to get it. He found the cub in the meadow. The little creature was unafraid of him. This wayward dog cub, who had evidently slipped into the water and been washed downstream a quarter of a mile from the place where he had been lying with his mother, was taken home and having been fondled there, was carried to the watcher's cottage. This was at five o'clock. The dam of our little otter was not speaking at that time; and the cub slept first on the bailiff's knee, next huddled on his host's shoulder underneath his coat, and last in a fish basket hung on a nail on the kitchen wall. It was a quarter past nine before I arrived to hear the watcher's story and to look at the cub and caress him. He was a nice little fellow, and when sleepily he yawned in our faces, the impulse to keep him was almost irresistible. But the temptation to capture a cub has always been put behind us, and we discussed how best to deal with our prize. We went outside to the river and we had our answer at once. Our little otter was calling to her lost cub. And so we put her son in a bed on the bank of the river at a place where the light from a gas lamp on the hill shone upon it, and crept back to an outbuilding to await developments. Either because he felt the change in the temperature or because he felt lonely, the cub began to squeak loudly. In less than three minutes the bitch, running like a ferret, bounded across the plank bridge over the mill lade to the box, drew back from it and returned to her hiding place. She repeated this movement five more times. On the last passage, she seized the cub by the scruff of the neck and slipped down to the river to swim with him to the beild on the other bank. Mother and son were reunited.

George Muller

Communist bees
❧ MAY 1931 ☙

Maeterlinck, like the early philosophers, saw in the hive-bee community the ideal Socialistic state; each individual had work to do for the good of the whole, and each must be prepared to sacrifice everything, even life, in this service. In the older and more decrepit walls in my neighbourhood are apparent 'swarms' of bees, superficially resembling hive bees. These, like those which burrow in our walks and lawns, throwing up little piles of sand, are called 'solitary bees', and their social economy is more like ours than the inhabitants of the hive. They live in colonies and are sociable, rather than social, for each has its own home or dwelling and each minds its own business and cares nothing about the welfare of its neighbours. Recent warm and sunny days brought many out to work amongst the flowers and stock their burrows with pollen; lowered temperature and the rain of this weekend caused wholesale disaster. Numbed, they crawled feebly on the paths, and unheeding feet crushed out their feeble lives; but though the larva which will hatch in the half-stocked tunnel may perish because the parent failed to complete her work the community as a whole will not suffer from the many deaths. The communistic social insects and these solitary yet gregarious bees provide interesting lines of study for enthusiastic students of sociology.

Thomas Coward

A wife to the rescue
ᴄᴧ JULY 1932 ᔆᔆ

Supper was late, and I got up to look at the last sight of shine on the sea. There were the two great cats playing on the lawn; but their movements seemed strange, their shapes in the failing light had a curious slope of the shoulders – a rake forward. The two young badgers came near – just pleasantly cruising over the lawn on an early evening stroll. As I slipped out of the house they slipped under a patch of veronica bushes. But I saw them a few minutes later moving over the rocks at the back of the house, the white stripes on their masks enabling one to pick them out easily – dark grey badgers on dark grey granite, outlined against the lighter greys of sea and western sky.

It was a still, windless night, and in a few seconds I heard their rustling passage through the high bracken and heather below the pile of rocks. They were making their way down the moor to the old sett of many openings which must have been the home to countless generations of badgers.

Katherine Arnold Foster

A southerner goes north

AUGUST 1932

A southerner has the feeling that she must stretch her eyes among these wide Northumberland hills so as to miss nothing of the sweep of road or moor or great fields running up to the sky. And even the side roads are so often quite straight for a mile or two, hedgeless and delightfully switchbacked, that one gets an intoxicating exhilaration of space and movement if motoring. The heather just now looks as if a soft pink purple mixture had been poured over the hills, so smoothly and evenly it is spread, hardly broken sometimes at all by bracken or rock.

Then one can turn down to a stream, one's eyes no longer 'stretched', and play with the water, flooding some tributary with a carefully devised dam, watching the way the alders always take the right shape and how the rocks and moss arrange their decorations; this is occupation enough for the whole day.

But I must turn south again with some unsatisfied desire. I have smelt bog myrtle, played in streams, and return refreshed by the sight of this wide, large-scale country, but this time I've found no Grass of Parnassus – and for that alone I would come the three hundred miles up through England.

Katherine Arnold Foster

CHAPTER FOUR

After the Scotts

The long reign of C.P. Scott at the *Guardian* ended officially in 1929 after 57 years as editor, but he remained Governing Director and a constant presence at the shoulder of his successor, his eldest son Ted. The *Guardian* might be radical but it was also dynastic. Ted was 49 and it looked as though there were many more years to come with a Scott in charge of its journalism. That was not to be. Four months after C.P.'s death in January 1932 and his grand funeral in Manchester which brought the city centre to a halt, Ted took his 15-year-old son Richard out sailing on Windermere. They were getting to know the *Pimpernel*, a small yacht Ted had bought with the help of Arthur Ransome, who insisted on a craft designed for novices with buoyancy tanks which made her unsinkable. 'Don't go and get drowned until I am there to fish you out,' cabled Ransome from an assignment at Aleppo in Syria, after hearing in March that the purchase was done. On 22 April, a squall tipped the *Pimpernel* over. She did not sink, but while Richard sat on the hull – the recommended course of action – his father unwisely swam for the shore. He suffered heart failure or cramp or both and was drowned.

The shock was enormous and it reached the secluded world of the Country Diarists. The Scotts had been outdoor people, Ted a keen Lake District climber and his father fond of sculling on Ullswater and taking rural cycling tours with his friend Mrs LeJeune. The new editor William Crozier, appointed by Ted's younger brother and co-director John from a very limited field in a wholly unexpected crisis, was an unknown quantity. He was a *Guardian* man, on the paper for 30 years, but never part of the inner circle. He had been in sub-editing and news, rather than features, and only four months earlier, John Scott had described him in a private note as not being 'of an *MG* way of thinking'. Country Diarists such as Helena Swanwick wondered if they would be treated as marginalia and swept aside.

Their fears proved groundless. Although Crozier could show a dry and forbidding manner, he was not what he might appear. One of his first memos to northern news agencies asked them to make sure that they reported fully to the paper on every striking instance of the ill-treatment of animals that came before the courts. He was an early campaigner for a ban on circus animals. The Country Diary's strong following and the volume of letters from readers it stimulated also struck him forcefully, and he began to take pains in considering new recruits.

A good example of this was J.K. Adams, a young Oxford student who laid siege to the *Guardian* in the late 1930s in what became a protracted set of manoeuvres by both sides. The skirmishing tone was set when Adams wrote announcing himself as freshly graduated from Balliol but failed to specify the class of his degree. Crozier later discovered that this reticence hid a third – just short of failing – and drily wrote 'as I suspected' in a lukewarm note to the news editor about a possible fortnight's trial. 'Difficult to know how he would shape at the job apart from birds, but he might be worth trying,' he added; but he had in fact been struck by Adams' enthusiasm and the fact that there were only three counties he had yet to explore for birds. Adams' search for full-time work at Cross Street continued in vain until 1943; he was drafted as an aircraftsman second class and then invalided out to teach classics at Wellington public school. But he continued to send bird bulletins and Crozier finally took him on as part of the Country Diary team. 'You should know something about everything and everything about some things,' he advised. 'We had a man here once who wrote so well about the North Pole that people used to ask if his leaders were written by one of the contemporary explorers. As a matter of fact, I believe he had never been any further north than Edinburgh.'

The diarists' world meanwhile lost its doyen when Thomas Coward died in 1933 but there was no parallel with the turmoil at the *Guardian* after Ted Scott drowned. A successor had been groomed by Coward: the most assiduous of his many correspondents and fellow field-naturalists, Arnold Boyd, a retired Army major who patrolled the same beat in Cheshire from the sands of the Dee through Delamere Forest and round the extraordinary, eroded landscape of the salt mines at Nantwich. Boyd was a graceful and amusing writer with the sort of countryside knowledge which comes from a practical life. He kept pigs, bees, ducks, hens, an orchard and a colony of albino pond snails, describing in one diary how his hives of bees once swarmed erratically, flew off en masse and were only tracked down because one of his neighbours was a rugby three-quarter who managed to keep up with the insects all the way to their proposed new home.

Boyd's classic study *A Country Parish* gives an invaluable picture of his surroundings at Antrobus, near Nantwich, in the 1930s and 1940s. His *Guardian* diaries form a similar record; along with detailed accounts of animal and plant life in the Coward style, he brought in vignettes of country people's life and traditions and had strong views about declining agriculture. The failure of 1930s farmers to deal with docks and thistles as their forebears had done infuriated him. He was delighted when Crozier accepted a rural Cheshire saying from him as a filler: 'Your farmer mun treat your land like a baby: keep its face clean and its bottom dry.' He charted food prices and the effects of the Depression on the countryside, describing an encounter with unemployed men from Manchester who had been drafted to repair country lanes, complete with signs which appealed to his whimsical turn of mind: 'Men working dead slow'. He anticipated many modern conservation issues; among his notions was a non-political version of the Tory party's 'Primrose League'. Theirs was a dining club. His would prosecute the many people who came out of the Lancashire towns on spring weekends and dug up Cheshire's primroses for their gardens.

Boyd set an example for later diarists in moving about and adapting his diary to different surroundings. Although usually in Cheshire, he would sometimes pop up in Sweden attending a bird migration conference, or Morocco, where he was interested in the culling of turtle doves. Readers enjoyed this in the same way that they liked his unusual mixture of extremely close observation of English rural life with global scientific work. The classic example of this was the repeated arrival in his homely world of exhausted birds carrying rings from distant lands; even, after the outbreak of war, lands which no longer existed. A black-headed gull arrived from what had been Czechoslovakia, tagged with the new Nazi denomination 'Zone 5'. The war also brought Boyd his greatest writing challenge, when he was posted with the Cheshire Regiment to guard the Mersey beaches in the nervy 'invasion summer' of 1940.

Characteristically, his initial concern that readers would get poor value from these surroundings soon gave way to exploration of the vast, rectangular town park, the model for Central Park in New York, and buoyant diary intros such as: 'Every few days there is some fresh flower to be seen by the Birkenhead docks.' His gently optimistic tone explains why the diary meant so much to readers at times of crisis, in the way that Basil de Selincourt had described when he stopped being 'S'. But it was not an attitude that everyone shared. In April 1939 Helena Swanwick, who had campaigned throughout the 1930s for tolerance towards Germany because of the unfairness of the Versailles treaty, wrote a last bitter letter to the *Guardian*, which understood Nazism better and had never accepted her view. She would never write again for the paper, not even a Country Diary, she told Crozier, adding: 'I am old and hope soon to die.' Aged 86, she rallied to take in evacuees at her home in Maidenhead but lost heart again before the end of the year and died in November from a deliberate overdose of sleeping tablets.

Getting used to planes
⚬ JULY 1933 ⚬

Aeroplanes have become a commonplace to most of us, and may pass overhead without causing an upward glance, but birds have not yet learned that these big 'hawks' are harmless. I was standing in my orchard, where a number of hand-reared and pinioned mallards live, when suddenly they all ran at full speed across the grass and shot into their house; not till then did I notice that an aeroplane was just coming into view over the trees. A gosling, infected by their fears, did just the same, and they did not reappear till the aeroplane was long out of sight.

It reminded me of an incident that occurred some years ago. As we were watching several thousand duck on a great Midland reservoir an aeroplane flew over and every one of the duck rose into the air; shortly after they had settled down again a peregrine falcon came over without causing a tithe of the excitement, although it flew straight through a 'spring' of teal and actually tried to strike one.

A small covert which lost its big trees early this year has now a greater profusion of the enchanter's nightshade than ever I remember to have seen. This plant, with its simple little spike of red buds and pale pink flowers, has a charm of its own, but hardly lives up to its rather high-sounding name.

Arnold Boyd

A cleaner London
⁓ AUGUST 1933 ⁓

I am in Westminster and I hope my country eye is not failing me. The trees seem to me as green and the sky as blue in London as they are in Oxfordshire, and perhaps they only seem so because I expect them to be black. Yet I do not think that is the explanation; I am convinced the air is far cleaner than it was twenty years ago. If that is so it is an achievement that does not affect London alone. The seagulls too, as they float on these town waters, and even the tame pelicans are pure white. Of course, I never before knew so much about waterfowl as I know now: which kind of duckling dives and which can only crane to the bottom and throw its tail in the air; and how long I should have had to wait before I heard young coots plaintively crying to be fed or saw the mother dive and share her booty with them. It is true that there is something slightly unromantic about these public performances. Watching a waterhen, stalking in the evening light along a bed of gladioli with sharp rhythmical thrusts of its sealing-wax bill, I almost thought for a moment that it must have borrowed some smart lady's lipstick; while the coot, with that conspicuous beak of Chinese white, explains, with melodramatic clearness, the virtue of a powdered nose.

Basil de Selincourt

Unhappy landing

SEPTEMBER 1933

A few days ago an unfortunate kingfisher was discovered alive in Manchester in extraordinary circumstances. It had dived into a tank of heavy oil at a gasworks, a mortal error that is difficult to understand. Kingfishers are notoriously prone to kill themselves against windows, misled undoubtedly by reflections, but these can hardly have caused the disaster this time; indeed, no more plausible theory has been suggested than the rather ribald one that the bird had acquired a liking for sardines. It was taken to a friend, who washed it in hot water and soda, and forced it to eat several meal-worms, and it so far recovered that it sat up and preened itself and actually whistled several times, but after living for some hours it suddenly toppled over and died. The oil had been too much for it.

It is seldom realised that the kingfisher is not uncommon near and even in Manchester, where it often visits Platt Fields; and it can also be seen regularly on or near the Irwell at Agecroft and has, indeed, recently nested there. In a land of meres and streams like Cheshire it is plentiful.

Arnold Boyd

Spyin' out

OCTOBER 1933

To the small Cheshire boy the bird-watcher is a source of abiding interest, and his field-glasses and telescope are invariably known as 'spying-glasses'. I was watching some gulls through my telescope when I became aware of a little boy with a dirty face and a close-cropped, almost shaven head, whose principal garment was a pair of someone else's trousers cut down; a delightful child, whose company was to enthral me for the next half-hour. A small friend called him to go and play, but he very properly replied: 'Naw, I'm watchin' this feller spyin' out' and attached himself to me.

We walked along the water's edge and he told me all about the gulls and duck that came there, and how sometimes he escorted 'our Eunice', too small to be safe by herself, to feed the swans; and then, still sticking to natural history, he became really excited on the subject of rats and the size of those where he lived, for he evidently knew them only too well. He had read the 'Pied Piper' at school, and the story had thrilled him to the very marrow. He grew quite breathless as he told the tale: how the rats were led away and how later on the children also were ''ticed into a big 'ole, but there was a lickle lame un as couldn't get in; an' all their muvvers was SHOUTin' 'em.' At least one part of his work at school had aroused his full interest.

Arnold Boyd

Under the stars
❧ JANUARY 1934 ☙

Walking by starlight is one of the joys of the country that the townsman can seldom share. Municipal councils and sub-committees for lighting see to that. Why, in the town one can be unaware of the moon, and a full moon at that, not to speak of the stars. And walking by starlight is not a bit like walking by moonlight either. It has a magic of its own. The bright, scintillating spears of starlight give a sharper edge to the contrasting shadows than the soft, diffused light of the moon.

Our way back through the lanes after a village entertainment was clearly lit by the stars overhead or glittering between the bare, black branches of the trees. No need of a torch. The waning moon had just

Cloth cap and monocle: Arnold Boyd was at home with everyone everywhere

risen and looked like some distant conflagration, but the great half-circle of dull red added little to the light.

Yesterday in the dusk of a grey day we watched the bright brown leaves that still clothe the beech scrub in the woods and the darker floor of sodden red mysteriously take on a warmer glow at sunset-time, though no sun was to be seen and there was very little colour in the sky. Hundreds of wood pigeons rose with a clatter from the trees and swept across the sky, little black silhouettes except for a few late stragglers whose soft grey was plainly visible as they rose or sank in front of the dark fir trees.

Janet Case

Wrong-footed
❧ JULY 1934 ☙

The breezy poster 'Llandudno Calling', which is to be seen on many railway stations, shows in the foreground a herring gull with a pair of yellow legs. Now the legs of our herring gulls are pinkish in colour; it is the lesser black-backed gull that has yellow legs, and it is necessary to go to the south of Europe or eastern Scandinavia to find a species of herring gull with legs of that colour. The staff of at least one station on the Cheshire lines, with a very proper zeal and a commendable love of accuracy, have used chalk to put matters right, and their herring gull is now standing on its own pink legs. Other stations please copy.

Arnold Boyd

Pass the onion
❧ NOVEMBER 1934 ☙

The belief that an onion can prevent the spread of infectious or contagious disease is firmly held still in rural Cheshire. An old country woman of my acquaintance, who died recently, was accustomed to peel an onion and place it on the mantelshelf whenever there was an epidemic of measles, scarlet fever or the like. She told me of its efficiency during a serious smallpox epidemic years ago. An onion was hung over the door of the post office in Stockton Heath, and though people were going in and out every day, nobody in the house caught the disease. After the epidemic had died out the onion was taken down, and it was all pitted with marks; as they said: 'All the smallpox had flown straight to the onion.'

Arnold Boyd

Crackshot with the rockery

MARCH 1935

A lady in Didsbury feeds the birds in her garden, and she and her small daughter derive much pleasure from their company, but when a kestrel came down from the sky and seized a little hen chaffinch in its talons it was more than she could stand. Running into the garden, she seized a chunk of the rockery, and with rapid and accurate aim slew the kestrel, a feat of which not every man — not even every cricketer — would have been capable. The kestrel was handed over for examination, and proved to be a real town-dweller — it was covered with soot. But in spite of its shabbiness it was, in another sense, a really clean bird, for only one parasite was found on it, instead of the hordes that most birds carry. There is evidently something to be said for soot.

Arnold Boyd

Oh for a bypass

MAY 1935

Much of the charm of the little gardens in the nearby Surrey village is due to the sense of mystery conveyed by the high walls that enclose them. The narrow, twisting street is bounded on either side by these old walls and only the lilac and mock orange trees showing over the top give a hint of the beauty inside. Here and there a perfect cottage garden is revealed by the ending of the wall or by a door in the wall left open, showing the peace, colour and security within. There is much talk of removing these ancient walls to 'straighten' the street so that the London traffic may rush through, unchecked in speed, from town to town. Although many of the gardens may be saved, their mystery will be lost, and their peaceful security will give place to dust, noise and speeding Londoners.

Passing through a new suburb of London recently I noticed that the tiny front gardens had been very charmingly planted with young elms, sycamores and poplars. All will be well for some years and the road will be pleasantly furnished, but in the end disaster will come, for either the rooms will be mournfully darkened and sunless or the owners will have to decide between disfiguring the trees in their prime by lopping, or by cutting them down at great expense. With such a wonderful variety of beautiful flowering shrubs and small trees so admirably suited to these positions, there is no need to turn to the grand forest trees, which essentially need broad acres for their setting.

MA

A seabird slum
❧ MAY 1935 ❧

The white cliffs of 'the island', scored with dark lines, soared above us; and on the narrow ledges as close as they could pack, tier above tier, we could see the serried lines of the guillemots, past all numbering. There were razorbills there too. A loud shout or a whistle from the boat would sometimes send them flying like a cloud of flies, only to line up again the moment after. Some few stood solitary by a hole or crevice where an egg was laid, peering out as through an open door.

Cormorants flew by, carrying bits of building material in their bills. A group of puffins swooped down upon the water and wrangled over some delicate morsel hanging from a red-and-yellow bill. Herring gulls floated by, or stood by their nesting places looking out on the world from the natural grandstand of these precipitous cliffs, where the seabirds congregate and where – with what seems miraculous skill – the guillemots actually rest their eggs on these crowded and perilous knife-edges on the cliff face. The downland grass behind was flecked with yellow cowslips.

Janet Case

An early gastropub
❧ JULY 1936 ☙

Early this week I enjoyed my first dish of new peas, eaten, unexpectedly enough, at the table of a Sussex country inn. I was surprised not only to be given peas so comparatively early, but to have them cooked superlatively well and served correctly as a dish apart. I learnt later, and subsequently confirmed from the visitors' book, that this humble village inn was frequented by two of the most famous chefs of London. We are all familiar with growing peas in rows and supporting them with hazel boughs and hurdles, but in the garden attached to the inn they had said goodbye to such paraphernalia. Their custom, which is apparently widely spread in this part of Sussex, is to sow peas thinly amongst the potatoes and let the two grow together; in this way two crops are secured from the same piece of land and neither seems the worse for the association. On the contrary, I was told that both crops greatly benefited by the companionship. The peas protect the potatoes and to a certain extent the potato haulms protect the peas and prevent them falling down on to the earth. Also, there was a great saving in the quantity of seed sown. Anyway, the tangible results were excellent and I shall certainly try the experiment next year.

MA

Strong liquor
❧ JULY 1936 ☙

To what, I wonder, is owed the countryside's apparent immunity this year from its usual eruption of Dorothy Perkins roses? Is the popularity of those – to my thinking – unsympathetic pink-papery flowers really on the wane? The hawthorn is over and done; the wild roses washed out by the storms of rain. What catches the eye up and down the country is the exceptionally prolific display of the flat-footed bunches of elder blossom. Elderflower wine, like the rest of the old-fashioned wines, has gone out of fashion, but I was offered some the other day and found a taste of it sweet and refreshing, with a slight tang which it owed, I imagine, to the dash of white vinegar which, together with water and sugar, is all there is to it. An innocent drink, I was told, but improved by a fortnight's keeping. Not to my taste, I fancy! I am shy of those 'innocent' drinks, which are apt to be unexpectedly heady, and I know what happens to the home-brewed cider after leaving it to 'work' for a fortnight in the barrel. But each to his taste.

Janet Case

Starling post
❧ NOVEMBER 1936 ☙

We have fixed up a new and original bird-trap in the orchard (it would make Mr Heath Robinson jealous if he saw it), and this week the string that shuts it was pulled for the first time. There were thirty-seven starlings inside, which were soon ringed and released, but the interesting thing was that two of them already wore rings — one was from the Swedish coast 60 kilometres south of Gothenburg, where it was ringed as a youngster on June 3rd last, and the other from Leiden in Holland. Every year we get additional proof that many of our winter starlings are birds that breed in the Baltic countries and that part of Europe, but to find two of these birds among so comparatively small a number was both strange and encouraging. By coincidence I had received a letter from Leiden just half an hour earlier — a most unusual event for me. There seems to be some lack of economy among the Dutch, for the starling might well have borne both messages.

Arnold Boyd

Cain and Abel

MARCH 1937

Late one night I noticed a light still burning in the kitchen of the Herefordshire farmhouse where I live and I found my landlord, the farmer, shaking snow from his greatcoat and pulling off Wellingtons. I asked what the trouble was – but no, there was none, only lambing had just started and he had been bringing his ewes into the big fold-yard beside the barn. One of them had been in difficulties and when he got back to her after shutting up the others she was unconscious, but he had managed to get her up and take her with her two lambs to safety.

He was going to sit up all night, so I offered a drink against the cold, and over a revived fire we sat and talked. From the subject of shepherds – he had none because he had no cottage for him – we discussed other problems of labour. The fact that he had no cottage, he said, had lost him several young men just as they were becoming really useful. Naturally they wanted to marry and must find a job where a cottage was provided. There are two eighteen-year-old lads on the farm, one hard-working and clever, the other a real 'bumble-daw'. I said how unfair I thought it was, that their wages were fixed at the same figure. Oh yes, he said, they both received the same cash, but Jim, the bright one, owned a pig and four ewes, which the farmer kept for him; he was allowed to take the milkfloat into town sometimes, he was being taught to ride, and had even been allowed to take the pride of the stable – the horse which is to win the farmers' race at our point-to-point – round the jumps up behind the house. Evidently these things make a great difference, for Jim is always contented, and I am sure will not leave until he gets married.

CHDA

Flailing about
❧ DECEMBER 1937 ☙

Two old flails, the valued possessions of an aged labourer who has just died, were recently given to me and are now in the Manchester Museum where a collection of old and modern implements is being formed; and quite time, too, for (as I was assured by an authority) we know far less about the distribution of the various forms of agricultural implements in Britain than about the tools of the South Sea islanders! Flails have soon passed out of memory, and of eleven occupants of a Manchester office there were only one or two who had the least idea of what they were. I carried them in my hand to a waiting car, probably the first man for many a long year to walk through St Ann's Square, Manchester, with a flail in his hand. We tried to work out the odds against our meeting someone else with a similar burden.

Arnold Boyd

Trouble with tits 2
❧ JANUARY 1938 ☙

It is now some years since tom-tits first discovered the vulnerability of milk bottles left on suburban doorsteps and learned to perforate the lids so as to get a free meal. Their activities in some places have become notorious, and it almost appears that the early pioneers must have passed on the good news to their friends. This week a neighbour who lives in an isolated country house miles from any town watched a blue-tit peck through the cardboard centre in the cap of one of these bottles and eat the topmost layer of cream. Interest was at first predominant, but it soon changed to indignation, and the depleted bottle was brought indoors. To use cream for choking cats is a proverbial extravagance, and although a tom-tit's capacity is limited, it was thought that a lump of suet or coconut (neither of which is wanted for a human breakfast) should be luxury enough for any tit.

We know that some of these birds are resident in our garden the year through, and even now they are roosting in their nesting-boxes, but it is obvious to any observer that they wander about the country to some extent. New blue tits often come to my traps in winter, are ringed, and pass on; in a few months far more individuals are marked than can be seen on any one day, and among them there is sometimes a smoky, shabby town-dweller. Had this pilferer come from some town to corrupt our country manners, or was it one of our own which had fallen from grace and made an independent discovery?

Arnold Boyd

Murderous owls
MAY 1938

I saw the first fledgling this week, a thrush from a yew tree beside the front door looking cold and miserable in a very welcome shower of rain. From one of the upstairs windows we could look down into a blackbird's nest containing four nestlings with wide open beaks. Alas! They will never appear on the lawn with the thrush. One by one, a little owl has had them, in spite of the frantic efforts of the parents to drive it off.

A very painstaking report was published last year which did much to vindicate the character of the little owl, but even that report admitted that some of them do steal young birds. I venture to think that while the diet of most little owls may be beetles there are many of them which feed largely upon young birds at this time of year. Probably where they are too thick on the ground more of them turn to the form of food which they find more rewarding for their labours. If it were not for the fact that the little owls themselves have young, I should take my gun to the pair of marauders in my garden.

CHDA

Defying the drought
ᕘ MAY 1938 ᕔ

Plants make desperate efforts to keep going. In one corner bordering on my lawn in Maidenhead is a stag's horn sumach, along whose furry branches a month ago appeared tufts of crimson chenille. The frost of May 7 burnt these to tinder, but a week later the lawn was dotted, for a distance of sixteen feet from the tree, with fernlike sprays of crimson chenille. It was a temptation to leave them there for they were pretty. But it would not really be agreeable to have a sumach forest instead of a lawn, so we hardened our hearts and pulled out the sappy shoots. For the moment they are stiff and gay in a blue bowl filled with wet sand.

Nature contrives a rotation of weeds. When I entered upon a much-neglected plot the rampant crops were nettles, docks and plantain and thistles. These were followed by a great mass of black nightshade which being annual was easily scotched. Last year there was an invasion of the curious little Claytonia, whose stem runs through the round leaf. I had only known the pink-flowered variety and this white-flowered one was not worth its keep, for it sprawls over a foot. This year the grass is over-run with speedwell and the field forget-me-not which revel in the drought. Shepherd's purse is a curse. It comes to maturity from seed in ten days and especially affects beds of seedlings where it pretends to be something else till it has smothered the rightful children of the garden. I see there has been rain in Manchester. Lucky Manchester!

Helena Swanwick

Dark and light
❧ OCTOBER 1938 ☙

Those who have visited the contrasting cottages at the 'New Homes for Old' display at Olympia will have admired the airy charm of the new timber cottage designed for an agricultural labourer. It stands next to a derelict cottage which only a few weeks ago was inhabited by an agricultural labourer and his family. The living room of the slum cottage is dark, damp and cheerless; whilst that of the new house has a generous window running the whole length of the wall and the room is flooded with sunlight.

The interesting comment of a farmer friend was that he thought that those who spent a long day out in the open felt it a relief and comfort to return to a room that was subdued and even dark. An interesting comment, but perhaps long years of tradition of squalid conditions provide the correct answer. Anyway, his wife, who spends much of the day in the house, would be the healthier for brighter conditions.

Shortly we shall see a weekend country cottage built at Olympia for the town-dweller. Here the conditions are reversed, the desire of the tenant being to spend the maximum amount of time in the open air. The architect even proposes to build an open hearth on the outside wall of the house so that the townee may sit warmly outside on his patio late into the night.

MA

If only
❧ SEPTEMBER 1939 ☙

I cannot help thinking that if only Hitler had been an ornithologist, he would have put off the war until the autumn bird migration was over. I wonder if any of the friendly Germans whom we met last year at the International Ornithological Congress at Rouen feel as I do. That he should force us to waste the last week of August and the first fortnight of September in a uniform which we hoped we had discarded for good is really the final outrage. This morning I stopped for five minutes on a causeway between two pools and there I saw a ruff and snipe in scores and had the luck to spot a garganey flying with a spring of teal; just an inkling of what we are missing elsewhere in our favourite haunts.

A correspondent living in Didsbury has had quite the unusual fortune of seeing a Camberwell beauty (*Nymphalis antiopa*) flying into his garden. This butterfly is a real rarity, which occasionally comes to England as a migrant from the Continent (where my correspondent has seen numbers of them), but nowadays there is always a suspicion that an English-caught one may have been bred in England from an imported pupa and released. There are about twenty recorded instances of its appearance in Lancashire and Cheshire, but so far as I know, no recent ones. There was evidently a notable immigration in 1872 but since then the records are few.

Arnold Boyd

Farewell to the swallows
❧ SEPTEMBER 1939 ☙

The lights are going out all over Europe, but they are being relit in many a garden and olive grove all along the northern fringe of the African continent, for the small songsters which have graced our countryside during the summer months will now be well on their way to their winter quarters in the south. No doubt most of them will be silent, or at most will make use of those soft notes known to bird-watchers as sub-song. The earlier broods of swallows and

The outbreak of war in September 1939 is marked by the diary — and by panic in a village when someone blew a whistle late at night

house martins have gone; for some days they could be seen in numbers on the wires or skimming along the surface of the village beck, but now only a few late-breeding birds sweep up to nests beneath the eaves or into the cow-sheds or pigsties on the farms. There has been war even in our small garden, for the robins, in freshly moulted plumage, have been staking out their claims to winter territories. There have been intermittent bursts of song, much 'ticking' among the trees, and posturing of birds with head and tail cocked up in an attitude of aggression. No doubt, too, there have

83

been protests made to those seen flying over neutral territory. One bird which carries a metal ring is, I think, a bird of the year, for most of the older ones carry a coloured ring as well, indicating that they have visited the trap on more than one occasion. So far none of these has yet appeared.

Ronald Garnett

A spring song
⊷ SEPTEMBER 1939 ⊶

Percy pulled up all the bluebells
Wouldn't even leave a few bells
Spoiling other folks' enjoyment
That was Percy's chief employment.
But the Flora League's Committee
For such conduct had no pity
Put the plants to better uses
Drowned him in the bluebells' juices.
Now the sexton of his mercy
Pulls the bell for little Percy.

Arnold Boyd

A refugee from the Nazis
⊷ DECEMBER 1939 ⊶

Just after Munich a black-headed gull was picked up beside one of the meres bearing a ring which showed that it had been marked in Czechoslovakia. As I recorded in these notes at the time, it came from part of that unfortunate country known as 'Zone 5', but after the German occupation full data of the bird were at last obtained. Now another gull has been found within ten miles of the place where last year's bird was discovered: on its ring, which was issued from the museum in Prague, were the letters CSR (Czecho-Slovakian Republic), showing that even the birds of that country still carry evidence of their birthright. We shall probably have to wait till the end of the war before full details of date and locality of ringing become available. Ornithologists should be allowed to disregard man-made frontiers like the birds themselves, or at least to have a clearing house for information at Geneva or The Hague.

Arnold Boyd

CHAPTER FIVE

Beasts and Bombs

The whole of the 1940s were dominated by the greatest crisis the world had seen, devastating global warfare followed by the immense process of reconstruction. So it is instructive that an interest in natural history and the countryside not only survived these far more pressing affairs, but flourished. This was the case not only among people generally, where it might be dismissed as taking refuge in old and familiar things, but also at the very top. Between negotiations with Hitler, the British prime minister Neville Chamberlain kept a log of birds he had seen in central London. He was kept informed by civil servants about a family of long-tailed tits nesting at the Treasury and in 1938 took the trouble to send a note from Downing Street to the British Empire Naturalists' Association reporting a kestrel flying over the Foreign Office. After the war, his triumphant successor Sir Winston Churchill busied himself, among all manner of other projects from oil-painting to bricklaying, with an attempt to reintroduce the extinct black-veined white butterfly to Kent. He discussed installing butterfly-attracting 'fountains of honey and water' in Chartwell's rose garden, telling his entomological adviser L. Hugh Newman, known to radio listeners as 'the Butterfly Man of the BBC': 'Let me have your plan soon and let it be a plan of action.'

There were practical reasons for this all but universal interest, above all because of attacks on convoys by Nazi U-boats. Outdated farming meant that Britain was importing two-thirds of its food by 1939 so there was an emergency campaign to grow more at home with slogans which were to become famous, such as 'Dig for Victory'. The government published a knowledgeable little guide called *The Hedgerow Harvest* which opened the eyes of many to the uses of wild flowers. This was followed by the creation of County Herb Committees which enlisted volunteers to collect medicinal plants. More than 4,000 tonnes of herbs were picked during five years of war, the equivalent of 750 tonnes of the plants when dried. The smallest CHC in Rutland proudly recorded a harvest of four tonnes of belladonna leaf alone, which was then processed to make pain-relieving drugs. The entire rosehip tonic business developed from wartime herb-collecting and depended on volunteers for a decade afterwards.

All this activity naturally impinged on the world of the Country Diary, along with other incursions of the national crisis. One of the *Guardian*'s food writers, Ambrose Heath, did a stint on the column and gave the herb collectors their due. The editor William Crozier was meanwhile exercised by a Herod-like government order that house sparrows should be 'destroyed by all and sundry' as supposed pests on vital farm allotment crops. He enlisted the diarist J.K. Adams to write leaders on the topic after one of Crozier's senior lieutenants, J.L. Hammond, reported that 'an immense amount of damage was done near his home by evacuated children who were told to destroy the nests and eggs of the birds and who, of course, destroyed everything'.

Adams and his colleagues were lucky to continue with the Diary.

Paper rationing, another result of the U-boat attacks, shrank all newspapers and much of the regular content had to be ditched. In one of her last letters to the paper before she committed suicide, Helena Swanwick told Crozier: 'I suppose that it will not be long before you eliminate little extras like Country Diaries.' It is one of the greatest tributes to the importance of the column that he did not. The length was cut by a third to 200 words, presenting the writers with an even greater challenge to be sparing and to value every word, but the diary appeared every day and, pro rata, took up far more room in the slender eight-page *Guardian* than its 350-word successor does in the enormous papers of today.

The team of writers was reinforced during the decade by regular recruits, among them John Harrison in Penrith, John Lockett, who was another recruit from the reporters' room, and Gwendolen McBryde, who lived in a supposedly much-haunted farmhouse in Herefordshire to the delight of her friend M.R. James, the Provost of Eton and King's College, Cambridge. His specialist knowledge of the Old Testament and medieval theology had long been obscured by his fame as a writer of ghost stories, mostly set in ancient seats of learning. He developed this habit as one of a trio of young students with wild imaginations including his best friend, Gwendolen's husband James, who illustrated two ghost books before dying of appendicitis just a year after his marriage in 1903. The Provost became a trustee for Gwendolen's little daughter Jane, who was the inspiration – and first audience – for many of his mysteries. Gwendolen was very different from the illustrious academic. Described by James as 'an enthusiastic, chirrupy sort of person', she crashed about her estate in an ancient Land Rover and tried to write children's stories about cats. Sent 'The Adventures of a Kitten' for his comments in 1952, the *Guardian*'s editor A.P. Wadsworth replied cautiously: 'The pictures are charming but I am not sure that you tell the story simply enough and that the "plot" so to speak is really clear.'

Cats featured regularly in Mrs McBryde's diary, but she and her colleagues had more remarkable things to report. Initially, the emergencies of war seemed to hit natural history and rural conservation hard; most reservoirs were placed strictly off-limits, which played havoc with birdwatching. On the other hand the resulting concentration of birders in the fewer permitted areas produced much more detailed records for those places. In 1943 the short stretch of the Thames towpath between Hammersmith and Mortlake was used by 17 expert recorders 200 times on 144 different days, providing a matchless picture of species and movements. Another naturalist, C.P. Castell, spent 1940–4 studying the way life developed in a single bomb crater on Bookham Common. Picking up the idea, the director of Kew Gardens looked for new plants on bomb sites in London and found 126.

Nearer to the *Guardian*'s Manchester base, the Cheshire diarist Arnold Boyd described how the local night shift of the Observer Corps diverted themselves by keeping detailed timings of birdsong; in May 1940 they recorded a cuckoo starting to sing at 3.53 a.m., stopping after 17 minutes for a 7-minute rest and then singing again, uninterrupted, for 11 minutes. Such enthusiasm played a part in post-war reconstruction, which was slower but more practical than the hasty and misconceived 'homes for heroes' initiative after the First World War. In 1949 the long-awaited dream of past *Guardian* allies such as Canon Rawnsley of the National Trust and the mass-trespassing ramblers of Kinder Scout was realised in the 1949 National Parks and Access to the Countryside Act. Not only did this establish Britain's first national park in the Derbyshire Peak District, including Kinder, it also set up the Countryside Commission, the Nature Conservancy Council and a structure of wildlife and rural defence and management which completed the pioneering work of Charles Rothschild and *Guardian* Country Diarists such as Thomas Coward 30 years earlier.

Bull's-eye bombing
◈ AUGUST 1940 ◈

Two bombs which fell on a field in a rural district harmed nothing but the crops, but local indignation at this proof of Boche unscrupulousness was unbounded: 'Eh! Just fancy! Bang in the middle of Ford's clover root. These Jerries will stick at nothing.' The farmer is in no doubt about the value of what he grows, but he does not care for a bomb's help in digging for victory.

Another thing that greatly impressed the neighbourhood was that the two bombs 'fell in a dead straight line' on the ground; though how two of anything could fail to do that is hardly clear.

Arnold Boyd

Pozzie and burgoo
◈ OCTOBER 1940 ◈

Although the army in the first German war made some use of rhyming slang, it was not allowed to displace many of the old soldiers' words derived from service in India. Some of them, it is true, are still current; in the battalion in which I am now serving, porridge is always 'burgoo' and jam is 'pozzie', but instead of 'rooty and muckin' for bread and butter we hear of 'Uncle Ned' or 'strike me dead' and 'roll in the gutter'. The rot had begun twenty-five years ago. Tea was then almost always known as 'char', but even so I can well remember a sergeant's saying he had got some 'Tom Thumb in his i-diddle-dee' when he had scrounged some rum and put it in his tea. But 'looping the loop' for soup must be a new phrase; it is certainly prevalent today. 'I want some squad halt in my looping-the-loop' is the modern way of asking for salt in your soup.

Utter inconsequence has always marked this form of slang. There is no reason why 'pig's ear', any more than any other rhyme, should mean beer, but it has long been as well-known as 'apples and pears' for stairs. These latest additions, however, are more lunatic than ever. It seems strange that 'roll-in-the-gutter' should be in such demand that it has earned a place on our ration cards.

Arnold Boyd

Gone fishing
⬥ JUNE 1941 ⬥

Over the water-splash and up the sandy track on the moor I made my way. My intention was to fish the stream for trout. When I reached the river heat already seemed to dance over the water and it was hopelessly clear. In amber patches of light fish could be seen cruising gently. I crept down the bank and waded upstream to where I could cast by a bit of broken water; I had seen an occasional rise. Midges danced over me. The mayfly orgy is over and has left the fish far from hungry. I had an inquiry or two, and now I had hooked my fish. All went well; but my next one gave a jump, a gleam, and he was free. I looked up. A young red squirrel was sat comfortably watching me from a shady oak. The yellow broom blazed in the sun; a perfect day, but not for fishing.

Gwen McBryde

This diary shows the close attention paid to the column by the editor Crozier; he sent a copy to McBryde underlining the word 'sat' in pencil and complaining that the tense (although a good Yorkshire usage) was grammatically wrong.

Another sort of war
⬥ SEPTEMBER 1941 ⬥

I sat in front of the hive watching a battle between the bees and marauding wasps. The doorway had been narrowed to help the defence, and across the entrance a line of bees was drawn up shoulder to shoulder with reserves just behind. On the alighting board in front of the main body were outposts or skirmishers to take the first shock of attack. 'Radgy' (bad-tempered) bees, so Jim, the local expert, says, get more honey than gentle ones, and certainly these became radgy enough at this attempt on their precious store. The outpost sentries at once engaged and often drove off the wasps as they arrived, but many reached, and some passed, the thin brown line in the doorway. A few got in and out again with their plunder, but sometimes a sort of rugby scrummage developed, and half-a-dozen bees emerged with a wasp rolled up in a ball and threw it to the ground, where it lay for a time, half-stupefied. One sentry displayed real soldierly conduct; he had been badly handled in an earlier action, but, when another wasp alighted beside him, pulled himself together and drove it off, only to collapse at the moment of victory.

Arnold Boyd

Filthy farms
ꙮ JULY 1942 ꙮ

Farmers have evidently forgotten the old saying: 'you can't have a clean farm with a dirty hedge' – to judge from the crop of thistles and cosk left untouched in many hedgerows. Some, although active enough to pull docks up, are too lazy to do more than throw them in a ditch instead of burying or burning them; one farmer, with plentiful lack of wit, cut his thistles last year, but only after they had seeded!

A friend has reported a 'scorched wing' (*Plagodis dolabraria*), a rarity in Cheshire, in June at Hale Barns, where this moth was found fifty or more years ago by a man who had been gardener to a well-known naturalist and became a first-rate entomologist himself.

Arnold Boyd

Spinning silk

Woolly bear caterpillars are to be seen hurrying across roads or toiling over rough ground in a great state of mind, looking for a suitable shelter in which to spin a cocoon. On the heather you may find the gigantic brilliant green caterpillar of the emperor moth. How often as a child I borrowed an unfortunate shooter's handkerchief in which to place one of these captives, and what beautiful moths were hatched from them!

A smell of damp cardboard carries me back to my nursery days when silkworms were the rage – or failing these any caterpillars served for pets, such as were easily found on the back of nasturtium leaves. I find, too, the smell of crushed nasturtium curiously reminiscent of those days – I cannot imagine how anyone can eat nasturtium leaves in salad. It is true that they are nice to handle, breaking apart in as pleasing a way as scones that are baked in foursomes. My brothers and I had quite a silkworm industry – we got as far as winding yellow silk on to reels. An attempt was made by my most advanced brother to harness the bobbin winder to his small steam engine.

Gwen McBryde

Birds and bombs

War is bringing changes to the wild life of the country. The appearance of an unusual bird or of abnormal numbers in times of active war will always be attributed to conditions abroad by those who seek an easy explanation. The fact is that disturbance caused by actual fighting and bombing is of very limited effect. One spring morning I went at daybreak to the craters made by a landmine and a big bomb during the night. By one a greenfinch went up and down in wavy breeding flight; on the lip of the larger crater a willow-wren sang its territorial song. Their alarm was short-lived.

It is rather the change in agriculture (which we hope will be permanent) and in game-preserving that brings about corresponding changes in the wild birds' status. I feared that last winter's widespread laying and cutting of the tall hedges, as arable replaced pasture, would drive away many of our turtle doves, and such was the case; never in the last twenty summers have I seen so few near my home. There are far fewer pheasants, for none are hand-reared now, but magpies, jays and crows flourish as never before. Foxes have been shot (though one took three of my pullets recently), but rats abound in the numerous wheatstacks. I was present with my terrier when a stack was threshed, and found old rats, half-grown and quite small ones together. One took refuge inside the trouser leg of a farm labourer, who was less amused than his fellow workers.

Arnold Boyd

The big metal hawks

❧ DECEMBER 1942 ❧

Birds, like ourselves, are rapidly becoming accustomed to aircraft (we may no longer call them aeroplanes), and seem hardly to notice what they once took for huge hawks. It was a very different state of things a few years ago. The geese and ducks in my orchard shot into their houses if an aircraft passed over; now they only look up. Not many years ago every duck of some 3,000 on a big reservoir in the Midlands flew high into the sky in their excitement when an aircraft passed the pool at a considerable height; and they took a long time to settle down again. Now it is only low-flying aircraft which cause even a mild alarm; a few duck, it is true, flew up when one skimmed the surface of the mere close to them a few days ago, but even they returned to the water at once, and the rest paid no heed whatever. Some bombing ranges, so I am told, have been deserted by the geese which normally winter there, but in others, to my own knowledge, the effect of intermittent bombing is more than counterbalanced by the fact that fishermen and ramblers keep clear of such places, and the duck enjoy more peace than they have for years.

Some of us remember the days when horses would hardly face a motor car, even when a red flag led the way. 'Custom reconciles us to every thing.'

Arnold Boyd

Spudulike
❧ OCTOBER 1943 ❧

Lord Woolton's wish that we should eat more potatoes has evidently been taken to heart in unexpected places. A dog of mine has developed a passion for them, and always makes straight for a potato field to find and eat any 'chats' (little ones) left lying there. A neighbour's cow choked and killed itself with a potato in its anxiety to do its bit. Another cow, 'blown' through eating too much clover, wandered to a marshy pasture and died before it could be dosed. It was, I believe, an old cow with 'more rings on its horns than there are groats in a black pudding', to use a local phrase, but a sad loss in these times. Cows put to graze on the eddish (aftermath) in even an ordinary hayfield are apt to become 'eddish-sick' because the new grass is too frim (tender); they require some of the harsher and drier herbage to make their diet wholesome.

Arnold Boyd

A short-lived mascot
◈ NOVEMBER 1943 ◈

A visitor to the coast of North Wales in August came across a gannet fast asleep on the beach, and, by creeping up silently, was able without arousing it to read the number on a ring which it wore on its leg. On inquiry I found that it had been ringed at Grassholm, off the coast of Pembroke, on July 16th 1938. It proved to be a quite well-known bird; it had been wounded in the wing and adopted by a detachment of the RAF who tried to keep it alive and christened it Charlie. I am sorry to say that Charlie did not long survive his injury.

Arnold Boyd

Quilts and bees
◈ JUNE 1944 ◈

I was talking to a woman whose mother lived to be 102. The old lady had a family of 13 and survived three of her children who died at over 60 years of age. She had three hobbies – chrysanthemums, bees and patchwork quilts. Whenever a grand-daughter was married, she was given one of the quilts. The patches were sewn on a blanket that was fixed on a wooden frame. The last quilt she made was composed of silk flags. These flags were at one time given in packets of cigarettes.

I believe her system of bee-keeping was on the old skep lines; the only attention the bees received was the gathering in of a swarm into an old umbrella, after which the bees were kept until the end of the season in an old box, or skep, and destroyed by sulphur and the honey taken. I feel she would not have enjoyed the taking of honey I had to do in May with the thermometer at 100, thunder brewing and the cross-bred brown bees in a very poor temper. There are so many wild bees in this district that the Italian queens have to be renewed every year.

Gwen McBryde

Harvest of the dump
ᐓ June 1944 ᐔ

A disused town dump in Northwich, now covered with vegetation, has produced this year a wonderful crop of the fungus known as the shaggy ink cap (*Coprinus comatus*). It is a tall, long, pale fungus with yellow patches, and like many other forms of life, including the human, it is infinitely more attractive in appearance when it is young. It is said to be edible, but later its gills turn black, and it deteriorates into an object of forbidding aspect. It is little wonder that it is never even considered as a possible food by the great majority, who enjoy and even pay large sums for the common mushroom.

Owing to the blackout few moths come indoors nowadays, but a white-tip clothes moth (*Trichophaga tapetzella*) flew in and settled on a wall. White-headed and with dark and whitish, oddly-shaped wings, which rise in a peak over the body, it resembles a bird-dropping. Its larvae feed on such things as rugs and skins, and I remember a big brood which emerged from an old forgotten horse-cloth thrown carelessly into a shippon corner. Fortunately it does not seem to be common in Cheshire, where it has been recorded from only two or three places.

Arnold Boyd

Victory through herbs
ᐓ July 1944 ᐔ

The old man paused by the yarrow to say, 'The finest herb that grows!' The Greeks knew the healing powers of *Achillea millefolium*, and it is valued by our folk, who call it 'thousandleaf' from the minutely cut feathery foliage. Its flowerheads bloom daintily, as a good example will show. Tight clustered buds open pin-points of white, furled rays which turn into cones that flatten to reveal disc florets, with their anthers bright gold at first. A few heads, however, are pink-tinged, others the rose of cultivated milfoil. Though dried as a brew for feverish colds, yarrow's use in salves seems to be obsolete.

Garden herbs need watching now. Harvested before flowering, when scent and leaf-texture are just right, their drying and storage are a pleasure. 'Digging for Victory' has encouraged interest in sweet pot-herbs with their musical names and individual savours, which link today with the Middle Ages, when herb gardens provided plants to improve food, to prevent disease (in theory at least), and to sweeten the carpet of rushes. Clumps of chives are a proof of this interest, for a few years ago many of the growers had never seen this herb.

Ambrose Heath

Mother's ruin

❧ AUGUST 1944 ❧

I went for a walk down a country lane with a small evacuee from Middlesex, who, like most children, took a great interest in wild flowers. We picked a bunch of between twenty and thirty different kinds – meadowsweet, bee-nettle, skullcap, enchanter's night-shade, yellow loosestrife and purple loosestrife, and other common flowers – but she refused to pick a bit of angelica, saying that it would break her mother's heart. Her mother explained later that she herself had been taught this odd belief in her child-hood. Evidently a superstition of this kind is widely held in England, for among the country people in this part of Cheshire 'kexes' (all the white umbelliferous flowers such as cow-parsley, chervil, hemlock, angelica etc.) are called 'mother-die', and some at least of the children dare not pick them for fear of killing their mothers.

Arnold Boyd

Farming's changing face
November 1944

A gradual change is taking place in many herds of Cheshire dairy cattle. At one time almost all were Shorthorns, and then British Friesians became popular, though Shorthorns are still in the great majority. In this neighbourhood there is one very successful herd of Guernseys, although most farmers regard Channel Island cattle as hardly robust enough for our climate. Now the Ayrshire is coming into favour, obviously Robert Louis Stevenson's 'friendly cow, all red and white', though we see little at present of the cream she 'gives with all her might, to eat with apple tart'. These cows are wonderful milkers, with long, capacious udders, and are reputed to be less prone to TB than any other breed. May their numbers increase!

Arnold Boyd

An American invader
March 1945

The destructive American grey squirrel seems to be on the increase again in this part of Cheshire. There is little first-hand evidence that they kill the native red squirrel, but two keeper friends of mine actually saw it happen, and their report coincides almost exactly with one recorded in Middleton's book, *The Grey Squirrel*. They heard squealing at the top of a big yew and watched three young red squirrels fall from the tree, each bitten at the back of the neck after the manner of a stoat's bite; the aggressor, a grey squirrel, was shot as it left the nest.

A pair of kestrels on the 13th gave a good performance of their display. They flew round in small circles one above the other with tails expanded wide; one of them occasionally flew with unusually rapid short wing-beats and all the time a continual 'ke-ke-ke' call was given and maintained when one of the pair settled on the topmost twig of a thorn bush.

Arnold Boyd

Happy campers
ᴊᴜʟʏ 1945

A word must be said about the visitors to our dales. The town and city folk sniff the pure mountain air delightedly as do hounds the sweet scent of otter. Their first exclamation is of delight in breathing the ozone rushing over the fells from east or west. After breakfast we see little of them until evening. The inns and farmhouses are packed, but after ten the hosts disperse. They are in the folds of the hills and not too frequently you come across companies little larger than those of the titlarks and wheatears you put up among the tussocks on the verges of trods and bracken on the screes. Only on the topmost cairns do they become for a while gregarious like jackdaws or rooks. What they see and hear on their journeyings is hardly less important and satisfactory than their fare at table. They take little with them on their climbs; moist jam sandwiches suffice, but they rejoice in the oatmeal porridge and eggs with rashers of bacon for breakfast and the soup and fish course, followed by sweets, fruit and custard for dinner. They acknowledge freely that they are on pasture good as that of the Herdwick sheep which leave the fells in autumn for the meadows in the low country.

George Muller

Prickly prey

OCTOBER 1946

A dog's attitude towards a hedgehog is usually stand-offish. My own Scottie can usually locate a virile or sleeping urchin from a distance of several yards, but she is content to display her cleverness by a vigorous barking and wagging of the tail and let well alone, and when her intelligence has been duly acknowledged she is satisfied to trot off to find something else. Not so all dogs, however. On Sunday we were skimming the countryside at a leisurely 30mph when we happened on an unusual spectacle, a black retriever trotting along with what at first appeared to be a bird's nest in its mouth. When we pulled up for investigation, the dog stopped too and laid down its capture, which turned out to be a rolled-up hedgehog with portions of its grass-and-leaf winter quarters adhering to the spines. The dog's owner came along and told us that his pet had a flair for hedgehogs. 'What does it do with them?' was the obvious query. 'Oh it just lays them down in the garden,' he answered. While the conversation was going on, the retriever with combined operations of muzzle and forefeet was turning the hedgehog over and over, and we were told, 'He always does that after he has put it down until he finds a position from which he can lift it again.' Frothing at the mouth, the dog persevered with his task, for some time without success. Then the owner, with a 'Come on lad' set off for home, and this command was a cue for the retriever to take drastic action – for the dog. He ceased the rollover process, picked up the bundle of prickles, and followed his master, his mobile tail giving evidence of complete satisfaction as he trotted along with his prize. The hedgehog was evidently in hibernation, for all this time it never unrolled nor gave any sign of life.

John Harrison

Gunpowder Gwen

❧ NOVEMBER 1946 ❧

Having to get the cultivation for next year's crops done at the same time as getting in this year's produce makes it difficult in autumn even when it is good weather. We have five different root crops being harvested as well as cider fruit and other apples and pears. I am glad that we have not got to deal with the big field of potatoes I saw yesterday. It was a dismal picture – fog and rain and rows of sodden bags of potatoes. The ground would have bogged anything but a tractor.

White frosts have wrecked the garden flowers. A wholesale clearance has had to be made and chrysanthemums alone are left. In the hedges bryony has hung out its bunches of glassy scarlet fruit. Long lines decked with even clusters stretch from branch to branch in hawthorn or twine down sprays of bramble. I regret that these truly spectacular decorations cannot be made use of.

I have been letting off fireworks for some very small children who have never seen any before. The little girl emerged reluctantly from the kitchen explaining that she had thought the cat mightn't like it. In my young days, the Fifth of November was a great night. One was hurried down the dark walk between the yew trees to an open field where the big bonfire was already alight. Catherine wheels spun and spluttered and rockets went up with a moan. All around you little demons rose from the ground, cracking, whirling, hopping. Some even emerged from the pond. And there was the lovely smell of gunpowder – precious stuff ordinarily; so hard to come by, when we needed it for our tiny cannon.

Gwen McBryde

The bombsites bloom
◈ APRIL 1947 ◈

Sunshine and warm south winds have worked a dramatic change on the face of the Surrey countryside in the past few days. One feels that this is no false spring and that her legions, having put to flight so harsh and bitter a winter, are now surging gloriously across the land and will receive no check. Down in the glades of the sunny woods several of our hibernating butterflies are already dancing. Peacocks, brimstones and tortoiseshells are there in plenty and I have seen two commas flitting about together high among the bare branches of an ancient oak. Finally they came to rest together on the underside of a branch, where, with their wings folded above their backs, they became almost indistinguishable from dry, old oak leaves.

The cuckoo has returned and his mellow call and the songs of skylarks, yellowhammers, tree pipits and of a common whitethroat are again part of the bird chorus. To a small copse beside the common, the blackcap has already returned. I watched him feeding on ivy berries as his song blended with those of the willow warblers and chiffchaffs and of our native thrushes and blackbirds. Even to the bomb-ruined acres of the City of London the black redstarts with their lovely russet and black plumage have returned, and if there are no primroses and celandines in those desolate wastes, the coltsfoot is making a brave show and carpeting many a pile of rubble with bright gold.

John Lockett

The flat rainbow
◈ JUNE 1948 ◈

A paradox in meteorological phenomena – a rainbow that was not a rain 'bow'! Heavy rain fell on Saturday as we set out for the field sports at Temple Sowerby – the 'queen of Westmorland villages' – but it cleared in the early afternoon, and we were able to watch the horse and pony racing and jumping, hound trails and wrestling in comparative comfort. Later in the afternoon, however, showers were falling on the Pennines and as we looked across to the range we beheld a horizontal 'rainbow' running for miles along the near top of England's backbone, with Knock, Dufton and Murton Pikes peeping above the upper line of the colour band. The area behind the purple strip had the appearance of an almost endless ribbon of heather in bloom. It must have been a rare occurrence for in over half a century's acquaintance with the Pennines, we had not seen it before. Idling home by the lanes we noted on Crowdundale beck – a boundary between Cumberland and Westmorland – numerous pied and grey wagtails aping the tactics of the spotted flycatcher as they rose, darted and twisted in the air to capture their 'supper'. While enjoying the delighted bubbling of the curlews in and above the meadows we watched a buzzard, at first being harried by a pair of black-headed gulls and then soaring spirally on seemingly motionless, outspread wings until it was lost to sight in a bank of fleecy cloud.

John Harrison

In the smoke
JANUARY 1949

As we were driving along the north side of Clapham Common this afternoon, we noticed a considerable number of black-headed gulls on the roofs of the adjoining houses. Some were lined up on the parapets, others were perched on chimneys from which no smoke was issuing, and a few were standing on smoking ones. It was noticeable that these last were all on the lee side of their chimneys, where they caught the full volume of the smoke as it blew over and about them. Herring gulls, rooks and starlings have also been seen perched on smoking chimneys like this, and it seems clear that they do so not merely for warmth but in order to obtain some benefit from the smoke. What that benefit is, however, one cannot with certainty say. Seeing how badly infected with parasites most birds are, it may be that their object in taking these smoke baths is to fumigate themselves. On the other hand, the smoke may have a pleasant effect on their skin. At all events, it would be interesting to know whether other birds have been seen indulging in this practice. We have given the common gulls that frequent the field opposite the house every opportunity of doing so by keeping the chimneys smoking well, but so far they have remained stiffly aloof.

J.K. Adams

CHAPTER SIX

New Recruits

In the autumn of 1951 an Essex schoolboy spent hours of his spare time climbing trees and scrabbling round on his hands and knees in Epping Forest for a project on how jays bury acorns to use as a winter food supply. Jim Chettleborough was an unqualified teenager, but his work was accepted as the first systematic study of a topic overlooked by professional ornithologists. It was typical of a decade which saw mass involvement in wildlife and countryside affairs grow as never before. The roots lay in the wartime herb committees, whose role was taken on and widened by a network of county natural history trusts. These had been pioneered back in the 1920s in Norfolk but only reached into the whole of the country after 1956 when a national coordinating group was formed. Its creation came in turn from an exercise started the previous year which saw 2,000 amateur botanists embark on the biggest survey ever undertaken of the country's wild plants. The British Isles were divided into 36-mile squares and data cards were sent in for all but ten of them; the resulting tally of 1,250,000 plant records was published as *The Atlas of British Flora* by Cambridge University Press and reckoned to be three-quarters of the maximum possible.

This amateur energy owed much to a new scale of interest in natural history in the media, particularly the broadcasting organisations which were starting to realise their unprecedented reach. Both the BBC and its new rival, independent television, started popular wildlife and countryside programmes, and in 1957 the BBC's Natural History Unit, which has since become deservedly famous, was founded in Bristol. Television was particularly eager because of the visual appeal of animals and beautiful landscape, but journalists everywhere sensed the value of 'green stories'. The unlikely subject of the melanistic variety of the peppered moth made headlines when the doctor and butterfly collector Sir Cyril Clarke statistically related its decline to the national rise in centenarians (recorded via telegrams from Buckingham Palace) as an index of declining pollution. When the BBC and the Council for Nature instituted a prize for natural history films, the first went to a programme on The Life History of the Alder Woodwasp and its Insect Enemies.

It was against this background that the *Guardian*'s Country Diaries were given new energy and significance in the paper, which was itself expanding after newsprint paper rationing was lifted. Their regular space moved from the back page to below the leader column, sharing prestigious room with the editor's own thoughts to which, in those days of a smaller but more influential readership, the country's leaders paid attention. Under A.P. Wadsworth and his rosy-faced fell-walking successor from 1956, Alistair Hetherington, the countryside had a favoured place, particularly when wildlife events lent a helping hand. In July 1951, for example, the Royal Entomological Society held a special meeting in the newspaper's home city to discuss the Manchester Moth, of which only three specimens have ever been captured. A *Guardian* leader hailed the insect as symbolising the fact that the city was not just a grimy centre of commercial success. 'We are not cotton-spinners all, sang Tennyson,' the leader-writer recalled. 'But he might have been a bit more respectful about these parts if he had known about our eminent moth.'

The paper's high command was also exercised about issues which the Country Diarists brought to their attention. A notable example was William Condry's repeated concern about farming practices and particularly pesticides, excessive use of artificial fertiliser and the destruction of hedges which led to the erosion of high-quality soil. Senior journalists also taxed diary writers about wildlife problems on their own doorsteps, or in one case, windowsills. Wadsworth conducted a lengthy correspondence with Arnold Boyd about the starlings which plagued Manchester city centre. 'Are central Birmingham's birds much the same as Manchester's and London's?' he asked before writing a leader on the subject, which ran alongside a report of a survey of starling infestation by boys at Bootham School in York.

The expertise of Boyd and Condry was meanwhile reinforced in the growing diary-writers group by two of the best-loved of the column's contributors in the last 50 years, both based in the Lake District. A. Harry Griffin reported fortnightly on Mondays from the felltops, where his climbing skills took him to places no other British journalist could reach; Enid (pronounced Ennid) Wilson was in charge of the valleys, every other week. Griffin was a journalist who cut his teeth in the 1930s on the *Daily Mail* in Manchester, then after the war got the plum job of Lake District man for the *Lancashire Evening Post* by going for interview in his wartime lieutenant-colonel's uniform, complete with medals, and overaweing the editor, whom he recalled as 'a little shit'. With his eagle's nose and crisp moustache, Griffin looked very much the retired military man, particularly as he grew ever more venerable until he wrote his final diary at the age of 93. But he was actually the son of a decorator in Barrow-in-Furness, whose most valuable

The doyen of the diarists: Harry Griffin died in harness aged 93
after contributing every other Monday without fail for 53 years

education after he left school at 15 was at the feet of the Oxbridge
academics who spent weekends at Wasdale Head mixing climbing
with passionate debates. Among strange subjects which lodged in
Harry's typical journalist's mind was a German professor's theory
that you should never dry yourself, because water re-entered the
body through skin pores and revitalised you. He got on at once
with the man who appointed him, A.P. Wadsworth, who –
uniquely among editors of the *Guardian* – had also left school at
15.

Enid was entirely different from the gregarious Griffin, so modest
that she insisted on her byline initials being reversed to WEJ. But she
had an equally harum-scarum background. Her father was the
famous Keswick rock-climber and photographer George Abraham
who liked to take her along when he tested cars to destruction for
motor companies on mountain roads. Enid went as ballast when her

father and Sandy Irvine, later lost on Mount Everest with George Mallory, made the first return journey by car over the beetling Hardknott and Wrynose passes in the 1920s. Abraham also had interesting ways of testing his children. Enid recalled: 'He would put half a crown on top of a tricky boulder to encourage us to climb for it. It took me a long time to realise that no Abraham was going to put that sort of money on top of a rock if there was any danger of anyone getting it easily.'

Wilson and Griffin were immensely skilled in getting inside the whole fabric of the Lakes, human as well as animal, plant and landscape, and between them created a lasting memorial to one of the most beautiful parts of Britain. Griffin never missed an instalment between January 1952 and his death in 2004. Wilson had only two gaps, once when she was very ill in hospital and once on her husband's death. He was responsible for her appointment in 1950 when the two were having breakfast together in their farm under Blencathra, their children grown up and working away. Enid read out the day's Country Diary and her husband said: 'Why don't you do that?' Enid replied: 'I couldn't possibly. I've never done anything like that in my life.' Her husband said: 'Try.' She sent a couple of trial pieces off to A.P. Wadsworth who accepted her, in his terms, 'on probation'. In her unfailingly modest way, she said shortly before her death in 1988, 'I have been on probation ever since.'

Mrs Wilson had in abundance the naturalist's skill described by Viscount Grey of Falloden, the former foreign secretary famous for marking the outbreak of the First World War with the prophetic comment: 'The lights are going out all over Europe.' An international expert on birds, he wrote: 'If we sit down in some secluded spot, unobtrusive and still, we shall presently understand how much there is that as passers-by we never see.' This was exactly Enid's technique. She was described by a colleague as being as shyly elusive as the creatures she wrote about, and she explained her technique

with human subjects – ancient craftworkers, taciturn farmwork-
ers – simply. 'They sort of realise you're a fairly harmless person and
that's it.'

Enid Wilson was described by Peter Preston, the least overtly
involved in the Country Diary of the *Guardian*'s editors, as 'one of
the greatest living Englishwomen', during an internal inquest in
1988 into why the paper had failed to review her book of collected
diaries (a very common omission which also upset Harry Griffin
and several other diarists-turned-authors). A later note from Preston
to Enid after a crew from Border TV had been round the paper's
main office in London to gather colleagues' opinions for a docu-
mentary on her work is also illuminating, particularly because of his
relative detachment. He told her: 'There were many moving
speeches and I felt much cheered up.'

A diarist's debut

ꙮ DECEMBER 1950 ꙮ

A full moon is very important in the country as many of the hunt
balls and village 'dos' are arranged for then. As the old mole-
catcher crossed the farmyard the other evening he glanced at the
sky and remarked: 'Aye, t'parish lamp's lit,' and sure enough there
was the full moon shining brightly over Bull Cop. It was the night
of the Hunt Ball. It reminded me of Bottom enjoining his company
to 'find out moonshine' for the time of their play. The old mole-
catcher visits the farms, but the young son at this farm has his own
very successful methods. I am told that a long bramble put into a
mole's run will tangle in its fur and make it an easy victim, but have
never tried the method myself. One which he brought into the
farm kitchen hissed most furiously and tried to dig its way into the
flagged floor. The farm cat catches moles but how she does it is a
mystery.

Many of the wild creatures take advantage of moonshine, too; there was a heavy scent of fox in the early morning in the gorse thicket on the hill. It is infested with rabbits and such small beer and is a happy hunting ground for foxes. The gorse buds are swelling fast and there are one or two golden flowers already.

Enid Wilson

Hedgehogs on the prowl
❧ AUGUST 1951 ❧

Late the other evening, when the last swifts were screaming and the bats were flitting in and out among the trees, I heard a soft rustle at the bottom of a hedge in a garden in south-east London. Rats occasionally come into the garden from the adjacent railway embankment, and thinking I was about to see one I picked up a stick to hit it with. Presently, however, there appeared through a hole in the hedge not a rat but a hedgehog. Slowly, and with much sniffing and grunting, it made its way to a heap of compost nearby and proceeded to rootle among the bean stalks and rhubarb leaves in search of the fat slugs which gather there. Meanwhile I heard an even fainter rustle farther along the hedge. The author of this proved to be a young hedgehog, so inexperienced that it allowed me to pick it up and showed no inclination to run away when I put it down. I imagine that, apart from rats and mice, the hedgehog is London's commonest wild animal. It seems to be more abundant, at all events, than the grey squirrel, which one rarely sees far from the parks and woods of the outer suburbs, and which has appeared only once during the past five years in the garden where I saw the hedgehogs.

J.K. Adams

The egg men
ᏬᎳ APRIL 1952 ᏯᏃ

The cloak-and-dagger men of the fells, the egg-collectors, have been about their bold, bad business recently, so there will be fewer young ravens and peregrines in Lakeland this summer than nature had planned. Each weekend during the nesting season these men have been roping down overhangs to the wild eyries of these fine mountain birds and pocketing the whole clutch every time. Sometimes they are working for a collector from outside the district, often the eggs are sold for big money, and occasionally the man on the rope is an enthusiast interested only in the eggs, not the cash. No doubt some of them would prefer it to be noised abroad that the peregrine has forsaken the Lake District, but this is fortunately not so. The raven has been nesting in most of his usual 'stations' but we do not hear much of the 'red' raven nowadays. This was the fabulous bird which used to nest in a crag in Oxendale, at the head of Great Langdale, almost in the shadow of Crinkle Crags. She came back to the same wild spot, or near it, as ravens do, year after year, but unlike other ravens, she laid red-coloured eggs. I have seen, in a lamp-lit room, behind drawn curtains, 16 clutches of these eggs – probably the only collection of its kind in existence. Forty pounds would not buy just one of these clutches. When the glass lid was carefully taken off the tray I was not allowed to touch the eggs and scarcely allowed to breathe.

Harry Griffin

Yankee dawdle
ᏬᎳ SEPTEMBER 1952 ᏯᏃ

The Festival of Britain has attracted many American visitors, but the latest arrival from across the Atlantic chose a place far less salubrious than the South Bank for its feast. A yellowshank – a bird that breeds in Arctic America and winters in Argentina and Patagonia and has rarely been found in our islands – was seen on the 9th on a sewage farm. Later in the day, thanks to a kind message, I was able to admire its long, yellow legs, its dark wings, and the pattern of its back and tail and to compare it with the ruffs and redshanks that kept it company. We read recently of two American tourists who endured our diet for two days only and then left for home. Although other waders fed diligently in the sewage tanks, this yellowshank also thought little of the succulent dainties provided for it and was never seen to feed on that or the following day, when, after standing forlorn for a time, it died.

Arnold Boyd

The lonely fox-trap
APRIL 1953

The return of the cold weather has thrown a fresh covering of snow over the tops and yesterday hail bounced on the new green tassels of the larches and trickled through the needles of the Scots firs. The water lay in hollows at the foot of the scree and the red flower cones of the bog myrtle were ready to open. I had gone to look at none of these things but to find an ancient fox-trap which stands a little way up the scree. No one ever goes there now, but I am told that sixty years ago it was in use and most of its strong wall still survives. It is built cleverly beside a great boulder which runs in from the scree to make a platform from which a hungry fox could look down into the trap, and is a massive and curious thing of dry walling, starting with big boulders and finishing with smaller stones and slabs above. It is about 12 feet across at the ground level, tapering with a batter on the wall to much less at the top; even the boulder leans inwards at its edge and the whole height is 10 feet. An old hen used to be put in and fed on corn. Presumably, scenting it, the fox would sniff round the outside, walk on to the platform and jump down inside, only to find that the overhang prevented any escape. I have often passed near the old trap and did not know of its existence; the maze of rocks and the tangle of trees hide it so well. I have never seen another like it in these valleys.

Enid Wilson

War on the ants
❧ APRIL 1953 ❧

A very rough estimate of the number of ants in my lawn is anything between 10,000 and, say, half a million. There certainly seem to be many more than there were last year, in spite of a systematic slaughter which went on for months. For some reason, ants prefer my lawn to those of any of my neighbours, which are completely ant-free. Perhaps my grass is more succulent or the underlying soil more suitable for burrowing purposes. Every type of powder designed for the extermination of ants has been tried but no matter what their losses, they come back refreshed, in greater numbers, to wreak their daily havoc. Is it possible, I sometimes wonder, that ants can get so accustomed to deadly powders that in time they can actually thrive on them? One powder I tried was of a very special type. It was said that it paralysed the ants so that they lost their senses and, instead of escaping, foolishly entered into the heaviest concentrations and ultimately perished. Rather like the elaborate machines for killing flies, once you have caught them, but I had reached the state in which I was prepared to try anything. But the only effect the joke powder had on my ants was to give them such perspicacity that they could be seen, great droves of them, carrying their eggs to safety and even dragging off their unconscious comrades, presumably to apply artificial respiration in some subterranean hideout. The next thing I tried, in desperation, was boiling water, which killed off the ants all right, but also finished off the grass. This year the grass is coming back, and so are the ants – whole divisions of them and fatter than ever.

Harry Griffin

Then as now
❧ JULY 1976 ❧

Most gardeners are not in love with insects. They tolerate bees and butterflies and throw insecticides at the rest. Ants are among the commonest insects in our garden. But are they pests or not? Some gardeners swear they are. Investigating rock plants which looked miserable, they have found ants' nests disturbing the roots and perhaps poisoning them with formic acid. All the same my guess is that on balance the multitudinous presence of ants in our garden is as beneficial as earthworms or falling leaves. What moves me to the defence of ants just now is something I saw this morning. I was looking out of the window when a lovely female green woodpecker flew down to the lawn closely followed by a young one. Mother woodpecker went straight to an ants' nest, filled her beak with ants with astonishing speed and then shovelled the whole lot into her infant's mouth. It was a charming scene which would not have been possible in a garden where ants are destroyed. There'll be a similar happening next month when the flying ants come out and rise heavenwards in their thousands. Mysteriously appearing from nowhere, the black-headed gulls will circle silently and gracefully about the sky, skilfully snapping up these tasty insects. But I fear my entomological friends will rebuke me for being so enthusiastic about the death of so many ants. Quite properly they could point out that most wonderful of all are the ants themselves and their social organisation worked out millions of years ago and still superior to anything man has yet devised.

William Condry

Eels and seals
ᔌ MAY 1954 ᔍ

Whether seals are short-sighted I do not know, but those to be seen on the coast of North Devon behave as though they were. If one stands and looks down on them from the top of a cliff, whence they might easily be mistaken for bathers treading water, they peer intently at one, dive, come up a few yards closer inshore, stare again, and repeat the process until, their shyness having overcome their curiosity, they disappear for good. At close quarters they look rather like large and playful dalmatian dogs swimming in the water, but when they have caught a fish they are anything but playful. Every fisherman knows how difficult an eel is to handle. To these seals it is child's play. One that caught a large conger brought it to a flat rock, held it down with its flippers, and skinned it as easily as if it had been undoing a zip-fastener. As creatures of character hereabouts they are equalled only by the ravens. Experience teaches adult ravens a certain wariness, but the young are disarmingly confiding. Two use a stretch of cliff-top along which I have been walking almost daily as their playground, and the procedure on my approach is always the same. Taking such bounding hops that one would think they were on springs, they make their way gradually to the cliff-edge, keeping an eye on me all the time, pause there until I am almost within reach of them, and then spread their wings and float out to sea with a backward glance that seems to say: 'Now try that one!'

J.K. Adams

Hands for sale
ᔌ NOVEMBER 1954 ᔍ

What a revolution has come about in half a century in the engagement of farm workers! When I was a junior reporter on a local paper one of my duties was to attend the Whitsuntide and Martinmas hirings to report fully on the 'state of the labour market', noting the rise or fall of wages of several 'grades' of workers. In those days the market-place was packed with farmers and their wives and men and women waiting to be 'hired' for the half-year. Most of the men carried a straw in their caps or mouths to indicate that they were open for engagement and not 'stoppin' on'. Bargaining was very close, and engagements were sealed by the payment of a shilling, called 'erls' – as binding as 'signed, sealed and dated'. Except for interim subs, wages were paid half-yearly; then the men got a new rig-out of clothing, paying for the previous half-year's, and leaving a new debt for six months!

Two major wars, the Agricultural Wages Act, the growth of mechanisation, and the coming of public transport have changed all that. I visited the hiring place yesterday, and there were fewer than a dozen people there, and there did not appear to be any hiring. Most of the available men and all domestic servants are now engaged through newspaper advertisements, and public 'hiring' has probably disappeared for ever. The undignified sight of women and girls standing for hire was done away with some thirty years ago. In the old days the farm men rarely visited the town except at term time; now they come in on motor-cycle or bus several times a week.

John Harrison

London's countryside
December 1955

A walk in London of which I am particularly fond and never tire is that across the Thames from Waterloo Station to Aldwych. The river scene changes constantly and in spring, summer and autumn there are always swans – sometimes as many as 50 – near the bridge.

At low water their white grace seems strangely out of place on the filthy mud which is exposed near to where the refuse barges receive their unsavoury cargoes. In the winter the swans disappear for long periods and only two or three come back from time to time. Where they go I do not know. A few weeks ago, however, when I was crossing the bridge at nightfall I happened to look over the parapet when a flock of some 20 swans flew from under the bridge towards Westminster. Seen thus from above against the darkness of the water, the moving patterns of birds, all starkly white, gave me one of those moments of rare and striking beauty likely to remain in my memory for ever.

In the winter the variety of seagulls to be seen from the bridge increases, and I usually count on watching common gulls, herring and great black-backed gulls, as well as, of course, the ever-plentiful black-headed gulls. One cold day recently I noticed a great flock of these flying and screaming excitedly above the traffic in Coventry Street, Leicester Square, where some crumbs were being thrown out of a fourth-storey office window.

John Lockett

David and Goliath
December 1956

The robin is noted for its aggressive attitude towards other small birds and especially to members of its own species that trespass on its own territory. But the robin is brave as well as aggressive. A few days ago I was walking in late twilight under some holm oaks and heard the characteristic challenging chatter of a robin. I looked around to see what it was that was causing so much indignation. No cat in sight, but disturbed by my inquiry a brown owl flew out from the thick evergreen foliage of the holm oak above my head. The robin was after him like a small arrow of vengeance and actually struck the owl in the soft feathers under the tail, causing the owl to swerve. The robin after his attack came back to chatter his indignation. The owl perched at about fifty paces distant but soon flew away with the robin again in pursuit.

I have never seen an owl attack a small bird during daylight but I have often seen owls fluttering under the eves of stacks where small birds roost. Owls also look for small birds at night in thick foliage. The robin, with an instinctive understanding of the habits of his enemy, was making use of what light remained on a winter's afternoon. I am pretty sure that this particular robin roosts either in the holm oaks or in a nearby yew tree.

Elliot Grant Watson

A mouse's house
ᑏ JULY 1957 ᑐ

Once upon a time a girl in a fairy story travelled far in search of happiness, and came home to find it on her own doorstep. The same sort of thing has happened here for, because of a temporary incapacity, I have forsaken the fells for the confines of my own garden and I have learnt much in the last week.

The nine chaffinches who come to, and inside, my windows are becoming more easily definable as characters, varying from the aggressive crested cock to the most shy of this year's youngsters. I had not noticed until now the little shrew mouse living in the green-slate wall below the window. It seemed at first that she was interested in the chaffinches' crumbs but apparently she prefers slugs or a few aphids for which she searches with her delicate snout held high. She is building a nest in the wall and yesterday she collected fallen quince leaves, but today she has found the dying leaves of an *Iris stylosa* and these are greatly to her liking. She tears them with vigour, tugging and uttering squeaks of excitement – or maybe squeaks in encouragement of her own efforts. She has fallen on her back several times when a leaf has parted untimely and many times the chaffinches' sudden flight has sent her in terror to her refuge.

Perhaps, at last, I shall learn, too, what creature leaves a little pile of many-coloured moths' wings each night in the corner of the stone-floored porch.

Enid Wilson

Crashing about in the Land Rover
OCTOBER 1958

A gale from the north rained the apples down. Forest trees have not changed colour and are still very dark; the wild cherries are pushing up like little tongues of flame among the treetops; and the ancient chestnuts light up the evening in a golden glow. Roses are gay with their last blooms; soon we shall be dependent on the berries of Pyracanthus and Cotoneaster, and the common Barberry, which I like best of all with their waxlike fruit. I have some large bushes in outlying parts that I gather from.

Our corner of the world has been turning out champion plough-men. We have generations of workmen in local families; skill does not come from books or theory, any more than does the under-standing of stock.

On the farm good use has been made of the burst of sunshine; straw bales were rescued and ground is being prepared for crops. Timber hauling has made a remarkable mess of the drives and tracks on a nearby estate; had I not been to the rally for Land Rovers last year, I should have thought it rash to put the car at the jumps, but it is remarkable what these Land Rovers can do without damaging themselves.

Gwen McBryde

Farewell to Coniston record-breakers
❧ MAY 1959 ❧

The speed kings have finished with this lovely lake for ever – or so we are told – and Coniston water is left with its occasional patch of sail, its handful of rowing boats and its char. It has been a twenty-years-long story, this saga of record-breaking on one of the least spoiled of the English Lakes, but very soon, when the boathouse, the crews, caravans, the advertisements and the great ugly cranes have gone, there will be little to remind us of the adventure. Perhaps the little post at each end of the measured kilometre will be left, but that will be all. Years ago people used to complain about the noise – the peace of Lakeland was being disturbed – but their voices are no longer heard, and indeed, the explosions at the slate quarries are louder. The record-seekers have perhaps brought in their wake a touch of ugliness and vulgarity, but that will soon be forgotten, while the rare beauty of a silver-blue flash streaking like an arrow along the mirrored lake in the morning sunlight will long be remembered. Today this straggling almost Alpine village which 20 years ago welcomed the young man's father is a little sad, and not only because the golden egg has disappeared. A breath of the exciting, outside world had blown into the Fell country – and they liked it.

Harry Griffin

The last Shire
❧ NOVEMBER 1960 ❧

Till lately a splendid black draught horse lived in retirement in the fields about our house. He was stolid, monolithic, aloof, living much within his private, equine ruminations: an accepted feature of the landscape, like the rocks and trees among which he lived, and almost as unmoving. In winter he held himself stern to wind and took the weather as it came across the estuary marshes. In summer's heat he stood day after day upon a little hill for there he caught the fullest delight from whatever breeze was passing. Then a few weeks ago he took sick of a chronic foot complaint and it was deemed best to destroy him. So perished what could well be the last great shire horse ever to set foot in these fields, for hereabouts at least, these great, feathery-legged earth-shakers will soon seem as outlandish as dinosaurs.

We tend to forget, I think, not only how recently but how quickly the big farm horse was dispensed with. Though some tractors were in service during the First World War yet even till the mid-Thirties you could still evaluate a farm by the number of its horses. An eight-horse farm you held in fair respect. A sixteen-horse farm you spoke of almost with reverence. Yet only ten years later, the Second World War having virtually completed the mechanisation of our farms, you could scan a whole countryside in vain for a glimpse of a horse at work.

William Condry

Tall tales from the brochures
❧ FEBRUARY 1961 ❧

Surely one of the most curious of trades is that of writer of the holiday brochures which at this season are unloaded on to the public. I wonder who writes them, who has the nerve to be so outrageously over-praiseful of those places which people are annually cajoled into visiting?

Am I wrong to picture some poor cliché-haunted hack slaving away with *Roget's Thesaurus of English Words and Phrases* on his knee, grinding out truthless eulogies of places he has never seen? Unashamedly he hands out the same old super-hackneyed superlatives to convince us that it is at Barmouth or Llandudno that we shall find that perfection of beauty, climate and relaxation that, although we may not have hitherto realised it, we all need so desperately.

The weather at these places he can always recommend with particular confidence. For example, in a current publication we are informed that Aberystwyth has 'scarcely a rainy day from May to October'! Now if we did not know from unhappy experience what nonsense this is, a glance at the weather statistics would show us that the average rainfall reaches high peaks in both July and August on this coast. But I expect I am wrong about our author. Far from being a poor hack he is probably a very smart and prosperous hack who holidays in the rarely failing sunshine of Majorca while the rarely failing rains of summer beat upon the British coasts.

William Condry

On the edge of England
ꙮ OCTOBER 1962 ꙮ

The north Cumberland coast seems an empty, deserted place on this October morning with the tide far out across the scaurs of the Solway Firth, but a closer look shows how unreal this seeming emptiness is. Party after party of small birds – mostly larks – are migrating south along the foreshore, urged on by the cool northerly air, and the local skylarks, possibly feeling their territory threatened, attack them fiercely as they pass, singing with renewed vigour after each sally. The coast was scoured by the recent gales, and the turf of the foreshore is fresh and green; the leaves of the burnet rose are darkly crimson but in one place I found a spray of frail and almost scentless roses. There is some sea thrift still in flower and a little thyme, and, where the turf gives place to marram grass, the sea holly is almost over, but still keeps a flush of brilliant blue in its smaller leaves.

Again, where the grass gives place to sand, the saltwort is strongly green and the sea-rocket has violet flowers, but nothing has more colour than the small shingle, damp with dew, between the highest tide wrack and the usual tideline. It has been gathered by the sea from both sides of the Solway and is of every shade from palest amber to black. The gulls are asleep in the sun far out on the firm sand, but the curlews, oystercatchers and redshanks are all in search of food, and already in the sand and the rocks there is that almost imperceptible murmur which comes as the tide begins to run in. One must always remember that this place, so innocent seeming, is where the tide has always been said to 'come in like a galloping horse'.

Enid Wilson

On the trail of the stinking hellebore: Enid Wilson
plant-hunting in the Lake District

Swan lake
ᴄ᚛ᴗ OCTOBER 1963 ᚛ᴗᴐ

Sometimes a small happening, or set of happenings, will turn a time or a place upside down and make things seem out of joint. It was so for me by Rydal Lake one day this week on a perfect, still October afternoon when the plumy-headed reeds nodded softly along the lake. The willows shed their leaves gently and one could hear a party of coots – sounds travel far now – making cheerful, watery splashings where the river runs in, but the traffic – buses, cars and lorries – bustled purposefully past, oblivious, by necessity, of the beauty round them. In a long pause in the traffic a quite different sound began; it was the quiet honking of wild swans and there, in the still water, was a pair of whooper swans, the first of the winter. Maybe this was their first journey south on migration, for these most lovely of birds, immaculate and majestic, were very ill at ease. They sailed round one another, murmuring, bowing their heads and bending their long necks in a kind of swan-ballet but keeping very close to one another. One could imagine that they wondered what this small piece of water, edged with noise, could be. Suddenly, they had had enough and rose together, their dangling feet making spurts of white water as they went, to wheel up and over the fell. I saw them again a little later, dark in the evening sky over Easedale, and hoped that they would find water to their liking somewhere, or that other swans, more used to the present disquiet, would join them from the north. After all, swans must have come to Rydal before man did.

Enid Wilson

CHAPTER SEVEN

Silent Spring

The Country Diary entered the 1960s with the strongest team it had yet fielded, and a sense that its subject was becoming one of the most important facing the country and indeed the world. In the way that a single book can sometimes touch an international nerve, Rachel Carson's *Silent Spring* sent a shiver through the wider public as well as government ministries. The horrible sight of dead rabbits everywhere following the deliberate introduction of myxomatosis in the mid-1950s lingered in people's minds. More and more realised that it mattered if pesticides were killing useful animals as well as pests, or that topsoil blew away when hedges were grubbed up. This tone was gently sounded by Enid Wilson and intermittently rather fiercely by Harry Griffin, a practical man who sat on many committees for the better ordering of Lakeland. But its most consistent promoter was Bill Condry, whose diaries came in every other Saturday from Ynys Edwin, Eglwysfach, Machynlleth, a Welsh tongue-twister which the *Guardian* surprisingly got right, although it several times had to apologise for printing his middle name as Martin when it was actually Moreton.

Condry had a powerful sense of radicalism, in the diary tradition of Helena Swanwick and Will Arnold Foster, but came from working stock, which was still unusual for *Guardian* writers at the time. His father was a diamond-setter in Birmingham and Bill spoke with that city's accent all his life, even after 50 years in his adopted Wales. Condry senior and his wife were political activists, pacifists and supporters of Keir Hardie and members of the Independent Labour Party. They belonged to the Clarion movement's cycling and rambling clubs, whose members were instructed in their governing tract *Merrie England* by Robert Blatchford to base their approach to life on Thoreau's *Walden, or Life in the Woods*.

The book was published in 1893 and sold more than 2,000,000 copies, preaching a socialist, cooperative gospel combined with an emphasis on studying and enjoying nature which gave Condry an idyllic upbringing. He recalled in later life how he learned to find beauty on Birmingham's doorstep. 'There were still ploughlands out towards Tom Nocker's wood, where lapwings, partridges and yellowhammers were making their last stand. In the abandoned garden of a once genteel country house, a former goldfish pond was full of great crested newts. On roadside tree-trunks in September, we sometimes found the large, spike-tailed caterpillars of the lime and poplar hawkmoths. Nothing thrilled my infant mind more.' Fittingly, he wrote a good biography of Thoreau.

Condry was quickly on to *Silent Spring*, promoting it in a diary in January 1963 which unashamedly concluded: 'This book will, we pray, be a best-seller.' He returned again and again to the theme of misguided farming practices, and was an early advocate of retaining wilderness areas, promoting their expansion in his study of Snowdonia. This was published in the Collins New Naturalist series which played an important part in informing the public about wildlife

William Condry, a Brummie who made the landscape of North Wales his own

issues, and drew heavily on the Country Diary team. Arnold Boyd's *A Country Parish* was part of the series, as was Ted Ellis's *The Broads*. Meanwhile, through the generosity of a fellow naturalist, W.H. Mappin, Condry and his wife Penny lived for many years in an isolated cottage in the Ynys Hir nature reserve near Machynlleth which they treated as their own small wilderness. After his retirement from teaching Condry became its official warden. He developed a network of interesting Welsh friends including the poet R.S. Thomas, who was arrested with him while on a birdwatching holiday in France. The pair were unintentionally scanning an army base with their binoculars but got out of trouble when Thomas showed the soldiers his birding notes and explained that they were watching a 'woodchat shrike' which he then ticked off on their 'twitching' list. The French gave up trying to understand and let them go.

Condry was particularly respected as an authority on soils and joined forces with the *Guardian*'s leader-writers and respected economic specialists such as Harford Thomas to campaign against the government's proposed abolition of the National Soil Survey, a meticulous and invaluable but expensive exercise. It was this sort of quiet influence of the Country Diary which was celebrated by the paper on 30 April 1966, when one of the most important changes for the band of writers themselves was finally put in place. Since 1913, they had been locked in the world of initials, which were considered very much the respectable thing for the professional middle class – it was always T.A. Coward, A.W. Boyd or G.W. Muller, and Gwen McBryde was addressed in private letters from M.R. James, who was very fond of her, as 'Dear Mrs McBryde' for more than ten years after her husband's death. Now they emerged, blinking and in at least one case struggling furiously, from 62 years of either complete or relative anonymity and had their names printed in full.

As the writer Geoffrey Moorhouse, then a *Guardian* reporter, put it in a celebratory feature: 'With bylines having successfully invaded every other corner of the newspaper, there seems no point in preserving a half-fiction of anonymity here.' Thus, EAE was revealed as Ted Ellis, the keeper of natural history at Norwich Castle Museum, and BC as Brian Chugg, an artist and natural historian based in Devon. The effects were startling, according to Harry Griffin in the Lake District, who started getting comments in the streets of Kendal about his efforts, from people who hadn't previously sussed the identity of AHG. Even the most reluctant diarist, Enid Wilson, who had gone to the lengths of jumbling her initials to WEJ to remain hidden, grew to enjoy the recognition which came with proper accreditation of her work. Other new colleagues were John Talbot White, an expert naturalist and author of books about Sussex; L.P. Samuels, the latest in the unbroken line of Cheshire birdmen; and Harry Tegner from Northumberland. He was a founding member of the British Deer Society and omnivorously knowledgeable about his patch. He had, in bundles, the enthusiasm for his subject which *Guardian* editors particularly enjoyed. Typically, he jumped into his car when one of his many contacts phoned him to say that a mysterious, snakelike fish had been washed ashore near Alnwick. 'I got there as fast as I could,' he remembered, 'but Morpeth rural district council were faster.' Their workmen had dismembered the creature to keep the beach clean, but just enough was left for Tegner to identify it as a northern basking shark.

Full bylines seemed to encourage the diarists to speak more boldly. Condry was soon berating the spread of regimented conifers in previously wild valleys, by writing about 'wonderful schemes devised by bat-blind politicians who, though they tog themselves up in green suits, can still see no further than the nearest money bags'. Bill Campbell, although always kind and gentle, went for Oxfordshire county council over the careless spraying of road verges rich in wild flowers. Both writers were in keeping with the increasingly impatient tone of the *Guardian* and its readers on such subjects; but in one aspect of wildlife and the countryside some country diarists were out of step with an opinionated section of their readers. Just as George Muller had been the subject of an organised – and successful – campaign by anti-fox-hunters, so his successors started running into 'cruelty trouble'.

The problem was an old one: town or suburban dwellers tended to condemn some country practices as barbaric while country people considered the criticisms ignorant and sentimental. The divide has never been absolute, but most of the diarists would have ranged themselves with Muller, who considered some sort of control essential for most wild animals, and felt that responsible hunters knew and in most cases cared more about their prey than those coming to the subject largely at second hand. The dilemma reached an acute point in 1977 when Colin Luckhurst's diary about how to kill a young rabbit wounded by his son's air rifle caused an outraged correspondence. But that was life, as the diarist and novelist Elliot Grant Watson said, after he too was attacked over a diary from Devon which described a buzzard eating a pet dog. Questioned by the *Guardian*, he said that his gardener knew the owner of the dog and had confirmed the episode, telling of a 'masterly big hawk'. Grant Watson continued: 'No doubt the dog was eaten in the same way as a rabbit would be eaten. I spared the details for the sake of squeamish readers. But such incidents are part of the world we live in. Like it or not.'

The pesticide scourge
NOVEMBER 1964

Several correspondents have written to say that I draw too dark a picture of the general poisoning of the countryside by chemicals. They can tell of districts where quite a number of insects survive, and maintain that the increase in crop production justifies the practice of heavy crop dusting. I can report what I find in this district, that all animal and bird life is vastly reduced in meadows, woods and heathlands. In urban districts, including my own garden, the birds that have left the countryside congregate in larger numbers than before, and this for the simple reason that there is no insect life in the woods, and many people throw their scraps out into the gardens. That increase of crop production cannot be contested, if we concentrate on short-term issues, but in the long term a different conclusion may be forced on us; it is indeed at present contended that changes already on the way may destroy the possibility of knowing important patterns established through millions of years of evolution, and that new biological techniques will give new tools for constructive purposes. Many biological and agricultural authorities are seriously questioning the ruthless destruction of all creatures, whether considered pests or not, and are troubled by the human interest that has shifted from concern for the soul to concern for material existence alone. It may be that the death of nature is being rapidly promoted by the huge tonnage of chemicals that are being distributed in the air and on the soil without sufficient thought for the long-term issue.

Elliot Grant Watson

Butterflies and biting flies
November 1964

I have been astonished to hear on the BBC recently that this year has been a particularly good one for butterflies, especially the brightly coloured and conspicuous vanessids. This has certainly not been the case in my own district of Cheshire where, of the residents, I have not seen a single peacock and very few small tortoiseshells. As to the migrant species, I have seen no painted ladies, which have always been scarce, but in my garden there has been only one red admiral where a few years ago there would have been a dozen feasting upon the rotten pears or fluttering over the border. It would be interesting to hear whether Cheshire entomologists agree with the BBC's verdict.

I have been asked how it is that the common housefly bites in the autumn and at no other season. The answer is that the housefly, although unpleasant enough in other respects, is innocent in this particular one. The offender is the stable fly, *Stomoxys calcitrans*, which frequently enters houses in this season and is superficially so like the housefly as to be hardly distinguished from it.

Although litters of rabbits succeed one another rapidly from

February to September, I hear from a friend in Wilmslow that there are many more very young ones in the fields than is usually the case so late in the year. Another result, no doubt, of this remarkably warm weather.

L.P. Samuels

Botanical scratches
❧ MARCH 1965 ❧

An interest in wild plants and where they grow is not always a comfortable thing to have. Some of the wilder, rare plants come too early in the year, often in bitter weather, and survive in awkward places as one might expect in these days of all-invading traffic. Some even need, at times, to be cared for to one's own discomfort, as my stone-roughened hands and bramble-torn legs testify at present. These scars were the consequence of looking after two rare hellebores (relatives of the Christmas rose) which grow on opposite sides of a rocky limestone valley on the fringe of this district. One, the stinking hellebore, which I prefer to call setterwort, is a magnificent, branching, evergreen plant with fringed leaves and down-turned, pale green flowers edged with purple. It lives in an ash copse in a treacherous fall of limestone criss-crossed with militant brambles. Early gales had battered the plants so it seemed sensible, with the flowers opening, to prop them up for the early bees to visit so that seed could be set. The other side of the valley is gentler and here the other hellebore – green hellebore called felon grass in the north – thrives in the shelter of a wall. Today, however, I found much of the wall fallen and had to remove piles of rock before the brilliant green, almost leafless flowers could be found. This same wall which shelters the hellebore, shelters armies of snails which eat its seeds and spread them about, too, with the slime of their bodies – a comfortable and self-contained community.

Enid Wilson

Spiders and mice
❧ FEBRUARY 1966 ❦

Further to my remarks about people's fear of small creatures, a Liverpool reader reports that he has heard that people who dread mice have no fear of spiders, and vice versa. He says that although both he and his daughter are antipathetic to spiders they have no fear of mice; but his wife, who has no fear of spiders, cannot bear mice. He also makes the point that, regretfully aware of his own spider-fear, he made every effort to prevent his daughter from acquiring it. So although spiders sent shudders up and down his spine, he bravely used to invite his infant daughter to inspect spiders and their webs with him, and to use his words, 'Never did I let her see that I disliked the creatures.'

But in spite of these precautions, at about three years old the child suddenly showed fear of spiders, a fear she has retained ever since although she is now grown up and is a biologist. Therefore my correspondent concludes that there must be something innate in these phobias and that I was wrong last week in suggesting that they are mainly acquired by children imitating their parents. He also doubts if the correct teaching of nature study could have much effect on these phobias. Knowledge and appreciation of the spiders' webs, he says, have done nothing to eliminate the horror of spiders either for himself or his daughter. A sad conclusion this, if it is a true one.

William Condry

Paradise lost
❧ AUGUST 1966 ❦

Here in Hampshire, I can remember the rich fauna of the district of the Meon valley, lying between the North and South Downs. Naturalists such as Jefferies, Hudson and Edward Thomas have well described its wildlife. I have also my pictures of rabbits with early morning sunlight shining through their pink, semi-transparent ears. Badgers, stoats, weasels, moles, foxes and several kinds of mice were well-balanced in ecological pattern. Of birds there were kestrels, buzzards, sparrowhawks, owls and all the commoner birds we know so well, together with flocks of wheatears and goldfinches. In most suburban gardens, nightingales sang in Maytime. Of insects there were hundreds of thousands of species; fritillaries in their dancing flight, azure blues, holly blues, chalkhill blues, silver-spotted blues, brown argus and the closely-related Duke of Burgundy fritillary. There were still to be found white admirals; there were scores of peacocks and red admirals, and of moths, to name but a few, puss moths emerging from their self-constructed fastnesses on willows and poplars. There were hawkmoths, privet, poplar, lime, eyed, and the most beautiful clear-winged hawks and hummingbird hawks. In the grasses innumerable spiders, beetles and many kinds of wild bee; a great harmonious multitude that made for human beings, young and old, a living environment to stimulate appreciation. Such was the countryside a mere thirty years ago. This loveliness extended back through untold generations of men, touching the imagination of poets, Spenser and Shakespeare, and all men open to the then-unlimited beauty of these happy islands. Today there is a different picture.

Elliot Grant Watson

Spreading the plague
DECEMBER 1966

Now that foot-and-mouth disease is only one county away from here, my neighbour, looking out on thousands of starlings and hundreds of gulls and lapwing among his Herefords, must view the scene with some trepidation — particularly if he has just been informed by the farming reporter of his Sunday newspaper that 'It is generally accepted but so far unproved that the disease is carried by birds, principally starlings, and in coastal areas by seagulls.' On the face of it, the assumption seems logical; twice a year our island is invaded by species which have a marked preference for the company of cattle, and these have either come from or passed through areas of Europe where foot-and-mouth is endemic. On these grounds one would expect outbreaks to occur in the south with the arrival of yellow wagtails in April, and, on a much greater scale, with the arrival of starlings from the Baltic regions in autumn. But nothing resembling this pattern is revealed from a study of the very detailed statistics of epidemics in Britain. About fifteen years ago (in a review of a work by veterinarians who were plainly not ornithologists) Richard Fitter made it clear, from an analysis of the known facts, that the verdict was 'not likely' rather than 'not proven'. The most significant point in this review, highly suggestive that man (or his cargo) was the virus-carrier, was the fact that the scourge practically ceased with the curtailment of shipping during the war years – but starlings still plied to and fro across the North Sea.

W.D. Campbell

Reindeer on the ski-lift 1
FEBRUARY 1967

It didn't seem at all strange to discover a bedraggled reindeer sheltering from the storm just inside the entrance to the chair-lift the other day, for the wind was like a knife and the ski-runs like tilted ice-rinks. Of course he might merely have come in for the company – you could see his fellows higher up on the snowbound hillside – or he might have been hoping for the chance of something more succulent than the frozen heather roots these creatures seem to live on. But he wasn't very friendly, responding to a cautious stroking by an angry swing of the head, so I left him standing disconsolate by the ticket office and looking as if he'd lost both Father Christmas and his sledge. I suppose they're harmless enough although a notice further down the mountain warns 'Beware of Reindeer', but doesn't explain why. These were the only wildlife we saw in the hills during a wild week, except for the ptarmigan in their white winter plumage hurrying through the snow, and once a handsome pheasant strutting across the track through the Rothiemurchus pines. Indeed, there were days, so fierce the winds, when these popular slopes were even deserted by the humans who normally at this time of year swarm like ants, and one day, especially, when I seemed quite alone in the mountains. Ski-ing that day was out of the question – you needed ice-axe and crampons just to get across the runs – and the wind so strong on the plateau that it took you all your time to avoid being blown over the edge. But down by Lake Morlich in the late afternoon the wind suddenly dropped for half an hour, and there was the quiet splendour of purpling hills and a foreground of silvered loch with the birches and pines showing black against a golden sunset like a Chinese painting.

Harry Griffin

Why not more wine?
❧ APRIL 1967 ☙

The cultivation of the vine in the open for wine production is sadly neglected in England and even a conservatory vine seems to be something of a rarity. Although the climate of southern England bears comparison with that of many European vine-growing districts, it is only a thinly scattered band of enthusiasts who practise viticulture, even though historical records show it to have been fairly widespread as late as the seventeenth century.

One of these enthusiasts has a vineyard not far from here at

Beaulieu Manor and he recently auctioned a vintage of his rosé wine in London; on the other side of Hampshire another commercial vineyard is run at Hambledon. The Beaulieu yard interests me most, however, as it lies on land which until the dissolution of the monasteries was worked by the Cistercian monks of the foundation. During the Middle Ages the expertise of viniculture was concentrated amongst the monks and it is attractive to attribute the decline of the industry in England to the destruction of the monastic communities and the subsequent dispersal of technical skill. I learn that a sixth of an acre of land will produce grapes to make a vintage of almost 400 bottles. My garden will not spare that much room but I intend to plant two dozen vines this October, half Brandt and half Gamay stock, to test the feasibility of garden-scale production.

Colin Luckhurst

Bees and their keepers
ᴄ𝕽 MAY 1968 𝕽ᴐ

This is a good year for blossom, the foam of wild cherry is retreating from the valleys now but upon the fells even ancient and storm-scarred trees shine white, as white as the snow which today lies on the mountain-tops. All the garden bushes, currants, gooseberries and raspberries – are thick with flower or bud and this year, for the first time in many, the sparrows have left my cut-leafed Japanese maple untouched. They usually take the buds almost as soon as they show but perhaps this damp spring has made the difference. Broom and gorse are yellow, sycamore is coming to flower and soon there will be apple blossom. Indeed, this is the time of year – the awakening – when I miss my bees which I had kept for so long and parted with three years ago. I still feel a surge of excitement in a good blossom year and remember the contented hum of working hives just as I remember the kindliness of my fellow beekeepers. It seemed to me that bees, like other creatures, take after their owners – the over-careful, perhaps nervous ones have kittle or 'hot-footed' bees, while the happy, easy-going ones preside over quietly contented stocks. One jumpy beekeeper here kept a bottle of ammonia (much needed) in his hedge for his own and his neighbours' solace but one of the older bee-men by contrast went round the countryside to clover or to heather with teeming hives in his car boot and its interior humming with bees. But, as he said, he never went 'agin t'bees'; he did not (so far as I know) tell the bees of family events as beekeepers were reputed to do but he often said, 'Let t'bees tell you, go with them, not agin them.' That was, indeed, his philosophy of life – go with it, not 'agin it'.

Enid Wilson

Ghosts on the road
FEBRUARY 1969

The A1 north of Newcastle is at present undergoing an extensive operation so as to convert it into a high-speed modern motorway. The City and County of Newcastle upon Tyne has now spread its urban tentacles up to the old pit village of Seaton Burn where the country takes over. Driving towards the city on a cold, wet winter day the view is hardly inspiring. Early one morning on the way to Newcastle upon Tyne, in the near-darkness of a late winter dawn, the traffic was brought to a halt by a uniformed figure within the limits of Seaton Burn RDC. Through the quick flicker of the wind-screen wipers, the man who brought the car to a standstill looked like a sort of moon man, only he was pitch black instead of white. His skull hat was shining in the steady sleet, his face was coal-stained with great white orbs around the eyes. His clothes were dark in colour whilst his feet were shod in a pair of massive steel-tipped boots. The procession the pitman was guarding now began to file across the A1. Each animal had a man at its head all dressed exactly like the traffic controller. The creatures they led were a quite astonishing sight. Little fat dwarf quadrupeds each shaven to the skin, their manes hogged and their tails shorn so that they looked like the trunks of miniature elephants. The pit ponies were all harnessed and their eyes blinkered against the dangers of debris and sudden daylight. The file of men and ponies drifted steadily across the road from pit-head to pit-head. There were sixteen of them, queer creatures from the earth's bowels spewed out across the modern motorised highway like some undulating, mystical dragon.

Henry Tegner

The power of plants
⬥ APRIL 1969 ⬥

A blister has appeared in the footpath, and soon at this point a few frail spikes of an errant lily-of-the-valley will crack and lift a hand-sized fragment of two-inch-thick tarmac. The greyish-green rosette of white bryony at the bottom of the hedge is just showing its first ascending shoots, and within a short time these will be progressing upwards at the rate of six inches a day. Above the bryony, a pencil-thick shoot of sycamore, cut back only a few minutes ago, is already producing a steady drip of leaking sap. But, impressive as these annual releases of pent-up energy are, one can at least (however mysterious the actual mechanics involved) trace the power to its latent source – the stored-up reserves of food from last year's chemical activities; the few shoots of bryony, for example, arise from a hidden tap root as large as a flower-show parsnip. But, as a demonstrator of truly phenomenal root pressure, a weed still in the seedling stage and only so far a few inches high, far excels the established plants in comparative power. This is goosegrass (cleavers or 'sweethearts'), which, since it is an annual, can have no other food reserves than those contained in the seed. Yet if, as happened yesterday, one hoes on dry ground (particularly on pale chalky soil such as mine), the point of severance of each threadlike stem of goosegrass, before the day is out, becomes the centre of a dark, damp patch as large as a saucer.

W.D. Campbell

Reindeers on the ski-lift 2
AUGUST 1969

Watching the lone bull reindeer through my binoculars I thought how extraordinarily bovine he looked. He was to me a somewhat incongruous sight out there on the ski-slopes above Glenmore.

Most deer are graceful, lithe, highly strung creatures quite incapable of domestication, although it has been recorded that a wealthy, eccentric American millionaire once succeeded in harnessing a team of red deer hinds to a carriage with what object no one seems to know. Did he have a Christmas calendar in mind with himself installed as the driver instead of Father Nick? Reindeer with the somewhat resounding specific name of *Rangifer tarandus* are the only deer who are regularly trained to carry loads and draw sleds. In the circumpolar regions they take the place of cattle, and in doing so provide milk, meat and leather so that, perhaps, their bovine appearance is not entirely inappropriate. Reindeer, of the wild variety, once inhabited the British Isles in considerable numbers, for their bones and antlers have been discovered in caves, bogs and riverbeds in abundance.

That was about the middle of the twelfth century. Britain was reindeerless until the early 1800s when a certain Robert Traill brought two bulls and a cow reindeer from Archangel to Caithness. This attempt at colonisation failed, as did a number of subsequent ones in places as far apart as Northumberland, Perthshire and Fife. Where others have failed to establish *Rangifer tarandus*, the Reindeer Council of the United Kingdom has now succeeded in so doing, and the bull-reindeer I watched from the window of the ski-lift chalet on Cairn Gorm is but one member of a herd of some five dozen of these gaunt, grey arctic deer who now frequent the Grampian slopes.

Henry Tegner

Egg Pie and Scabharbour
OCTOBER 1970

Egg Pie Lane leads out of Scabharbour Lane and winds its narrow way through coppiced woods and unkempt hedgerows on steep clay banks. It is one of those lanes that conceals more than it reveals. The occasional wayside cottages stand half-hidden behind pond and orchard and the reddening chestnuts. In one of them, W.H. Davies lived for a short time in 1905. I try to imagine the conversations he had with Edward Thomas, the poet, who lived at nearby Elses Farm and encouraged Davies in his writing. Thomas spent two of the happiest years of his short life at the farm though he is not remembered in the district now. The place has hardly changed since he lived there. The small farmhouse built in Flemish bond, red and grey brick alternating, is set well back from the road, standing behind big black-timbered barns and two round oasts. Over the meadows to the north is seen the tall tower of St George's church, high on the hill above Sevenoaks Weald. Here are many of the images that the poet stored in his imagination and used later to celebrate his devotion to the rural scene. Some of Thomas's poems are almost incantations of country names. I wonder what he made of Egg Pie Lane and Scabharbour.

John T. White

The fatal light

ᘓ NOVEMBER 1970 ᘚ

Last week on Bardsey Island we had what is known there as a light-house night. As we walked through the darkness towards the lighthouse, we began to see a few birds overhead looking like silver balls as the beams caught them for a moment. At that range one might accept it as a rather attractive scene with the birds performing a graceful aerial ballet. Then the reality. You reach the foot of the lighthouse and look up and see that in fact there are thousands of birds up there. And that far from ballet dancing they are swirling round in a death struggle and are totally in the power of the blinding rays. The strong wind is full of their sharp cries and every few minutes you hear the crunch of a frail body striking the tower. Soon on the ground there are dead birds all about you. Or birds squatting in dazed unnatural positions. Or birds so damaged all you can do is despatch them. This is a slaughter that has been going on for years. But in spite of all the remedies that have been tried, it is evident that the answer has not yet been found. My feeling is that only a drastic alteration in the nature of the light itself can possibly reduce the casualties. Such a change can only be made by Trinity House. And maybe that will not happen till some of the Elder Brethren themselves have experienced a harrowing lighthouse night on Bardsey.

William Condry

The advantages of sex

ᘓ DECEMBER 1970 ᘚ

Some two hundred years ago, the Reverend Gilbert White, choosing his words with typical delicacy, made the observation that earthworms are 'much addicted to venery'. On many mornings recently, in spite of almost freezing temperatures, many pairs of earthworms, with their tail-ends in adjacent burrows, have been observed with their fore-parts 'locked in the ultimate embrace' on the surface not only of the lawn, but also of the bare earth. The operation is not, in fact, the passionate affair which White's coy description suggests – since earthworms are hermaphrodite, all that is taking place is the mutual exchange of sperms, which will later be used to fertilise the eggs laid in the leathery greenish-brown capsules. But the interest of this procedure is that for its sluggish duration – which may be for a whole day – the participants seem to become immune to the normally alarming advent of daylight; even more extraordinary seems to be the immunity from the attention of the early bird, traditionally apt to snatch the partially surfaced worm just before sunrise has had its warning effect on the light-sensitive skin. I have repeatedly noted one of my backdoor blackbirds, on its usual early morning patrol of the path outside, pass within a few foot or so of immobile and fully exposed earthworms, and leave them to it with (apparently) a chivalrous averting of the eye.

W.D. Campbell

Death on the dunes
ꙮ DECEMBER 1970 ꙮ

The rabbit men come a long way, from Nottingham, to undertake a clearance of the dunes at Gibraltar Point. They arrive in the pale light of early morning as the low angle of the sun's rays is clearing a thin mist and dispelling the white rime of the frost along the fenland edge of the Wash. On the line of dunes, honeycombed with rabbit warrens, they plan their strategy. One of their number, it is politely explained, is unable to join them on this occasion. It would be unwise to inquire about what has detained him – the alliance is patently an unholy one and poachers, even convicted ones, bring specialist skills to bear in this operation. A lean young whippet, grey and bright eyes, crouches beside them. It shivers with cold that is superseded by excitement as preparations are advanced. Its coat looks like velvet in the morning light and its bright eyes flicker nervously. It is well trained. Although a leaner and hungrier beast would be hard to find it remains still as the burrows are marked and nets set on lightly driven staves. When all is ready the leader of the group, warming his hands on a cupped cigarette and pulling his woollen hat well down, returns to the van for the ferrets. The nets are arranged to funnel emerging rabbits, panicked by the whippet, into a meshed corner. As the ferret disappears down the burrow all is still on the surface – intent faces watch the possible exits. There is a sudden activity – the bouncing emergence of a buck rabbit, the flash of a whippet and thud of a punch preface the deposit of the first inert body on the bank. And tomorrow a Nottingham butcher will be offering very fresh rabbit among his wares.

Colin Luckhurst

The old and the new
❧ MARCH 1971 ☙

Farmer Y is typical of one sort of Welsh farmer. Though still fairly young, he farms in an old tradition. He keeps close to his farm, working quietly at the daily tasks, goes to market only when really necessary, is a very Welsh-speaking, retiring, distant man, rather slow to smile. He is a contemplative individual, is knowledgeable about local history, and has a genuine respect for the land. And he still looks after his hedges, oblivious of the argument that so many miles of hedges are uneconomic. Day after day, for weeks past, he has been laying them with skill. He manages to keep abreast of the cost of living. But for how much longer? Then there is his neighbour, Farmer Z, a real man of business, a good mixer, likeable, restless, a Welshman always away at the English markets, constantly on his toes to do a deal. Not so much a farmer as a speculator, he uses his land as an overstocked ranch on which the animals roam half-wild and ill-tended, for none of them stay long under his quick turnover system. His land is taking a beating from all those hooves but he is making a fortune and laughs to see Farmer Y devoting weeks on end to so profitless a chore as hedging. I am afraid it cannot be long before most of the Farmer Ys will have sold out to the Farmer Zs. And there will be no more hedging.

William Condry

Outdoing Wimbledon
❧ JULY 1972 ❧

If ever in future I waste valuable hours of daylight by staying indoors to watch a tennis final on television I must remember to draw the curtains and screen off the world outside. Last week, during the ladies singles final, a chance visitor would have had doubts about my sanity or at least pity for the quality of my eyesight, for it would have appeared that, at a range of some four yards, I was watching the exciting proceedings through powerful binoculars. The true explanation is that a pair of goldfinches kept shuttling to and fro across my line of vision beyond the screen, and as such behaviour usually betrays nest-building activities, I had to determine the focal point of their journeys. However much the grace, determination and stamina of the human pair might have pleased an advocate of Women's Liberation, the alternative programme which I chose to view would have had the opposite effect, for obviously what was going on was one more example of the unfair status of the female even in the world of goldfinches. The male added colour and vocal encourage-ment to his mate, and dutifully accompanied her on every journey, but he did not bring back a morsel of cobweb or moss – although, to his credit, it must be admitted that he sang continuously and flirted his tail in an ecstasy of approval while his wife fashioned the tight little cup right at the apex of the small walnut tree in the paddock.

W.D. Campbell

Crossing the border

⟡ DECEMBER 1972 ⟡

It is always interesting to go over the Border into lowland Scotland and to see how, almost imperceptibly, the character of the land and even of the people and the animals changes. The true Debatable Land near the Border is poor, too many past wars have tended to keep it so and, anyhow, much of it was always a 'moss' (the home of the moss-troopers, outlaws of both sides) and much of it is still inclined to acid poverty. It is the sheep, to me, which especially mark the difference on each side of the Border. The rough-faced and the Herdwick sheep of Cumberland are apt to be dark in colour and to sink in the now snow-splotched fells. The true Cheviot sheep to the north are quite different in looks. The Cheviot hills are less rocky than the Cumbrian fells and are more rolling and greener, and the sheep who roam there stand out like big white and woolly toys against the green. They have, however, no other likeness at all to toys. It is noticeable how they stay together, especially on higher ground, and one Ettrick shepherd says they are 'hesseled', just as ours are 'heafed', and will always try to come back to it, even if driven away. A Cumberland farmer whose neighbour has introduced some Cheviots evidently respects them too. He speaks of them as being 'as wild as winter' and even worse ratchers than his Herdwicks – which is saying a lot. 'Let them,' he says, 'git their heids through owt and they're off – they just put their ears in the air and they go.' No one would think so to see them so settled and so douce-looking on their Cheviot slopes.

Enid Wilson

Beyond the marsh
❧ JANUARY 1973 ❧

It was winter at Hickling. The hamlet froze under a thick mist hanging over the Downs. The hedgerows were rich with rime, ivy leaves wore a crystalline halo, and the dead heads of hemlock flowered with frost. Icicles dripped from the barn where two men were cutting logs, their heavy breathing mingling with the cold air. The church was locked. I turned my back on it all and made my way downhill to the marshes at Lower Halstow. Only a handful of miles away, but it was another season. The wind riffled across the mudflats and the sun broke through. The sea dike pointed to clear skies as I walked along the land's edge where the sea aster was still in flower and the groundsel just opening. The air was full of the wheeling and chatter of oystercatchers, and far off on Ham Ouse a large flock of Brent geese took their ease. Occasionally a flight took off for a leisurely turn on the breeze, their deep honking adding a wilder note to the estuary's music. Gulls swooped and perched on the rotting ribs of wrecks trapped in the mud. Coastal craft were leaning drunkenly on the beds of creeks, and men were pottering happily with the mysteries of gear and tackle. In precarious safety behind the sea wall stood a small church with worn Saxon brickwork. I obtained the key at a nearby cottage and, on entering, found more marine memories. On one of the arches of the south aisle was a clear picture of a mediaeval ship tossing on the waves and, above it, a dark figure loomed with arms outstretched. This shore has claimed many a victim, but this was one of the days when it seemed a beckoning haven.

John T. White

CHAPTER EIGHT

Lunch in London

In 1974 the first and so far only lunch for Country Diarists was held by the *Guardian* at the Great Northern Hotel in London, hosted by the editor Alistair Hetherington, a great outdoors man who thought that it would be interesting to get these fresh-air colleagues together. No one was expecting a Fleet Street bacchanalia; the editor was almost as austere in his tastes as C.P. Scott, whose lunch at the Manchester office was invariably two hard-boiled eggs with a twist of salt, plus an apple or orange and a glass of milk. Hetherington was notorious for providing senior editorial conferences, in other national papers afloat on wine or spirits, with a choice of orange juice or water.

He first raised the idea of a beanfeast with Harry Griffin on a plod together up the Lake District mountain Ill Bell which the usually garrulous diarist remembered for years afterwards because the wind was so strong that many of the notions and complaints he tried to put to the editor went unheard. Hetherington then pursued his plan in an apologetic letter to William Condry about two different diaries appearing on the same day, one in the North and one in London – a common glitch at a time when copy transmission muddles between London and Manchester led to *Private Eye* nicknaming the paper the *Grauniad*. 'Is there in the ornithological or naturalists' calendar a day when a number of diarists might be coming to London?' he asked. 'It would be nice to meet them and give them a chance to meet each other.'

Condry suspected he was joking and replied ambivalently on 10 August 1973: 'What a splendid idea to invite your country bumpkin country diarists up to London for lunch! I bet some of us have never been to London in our lives. I have but not often and not for years. I think I could find my way over Kilimanjaro but am helpless in a town. It will be quite an adventure for us but my wife will tie a label to me with my address on it.' There were no wildlife or countryside conferences due, he added, 'so I am afraid that if you want to get us all together it will have to be a special Country Diarists Conference, Summer School, Symposium, Briefing, Seminar, Sit-in, Love-in or similar unlikely arrangement. But it was a nice thought.'

In spite of his scepticism, the plan was realised. All the participants but one are now dead but Griffin remembered it years later, including the unexpected appearance of alcohol and the way the diarists had to line up for a group photograph. 'Perhaps they thought we would have straw in our hair, but I seem to remember we appeared pretty ordinary, although on the elderly side,' he wrote in an article marking his half-century as a contributor in 2000, when he was 90. 'But the talk over the wine was certainly wide-ranging and it was a rare chance, for me at least, to get a whiff of city air.' The guests included the column's subeditors, who were left in no doubt about the effects of cutting payoff lines to make room for other pieces in the paper, and a young feature-writer, Janet Watts, who described the event in the next day's *Guardian*.

She still remembers an atmosphere of pipes and nostalgia (Enid Wilson was the only other woman present) and the way that the diarists kept up their instinctive observing skills. One of them was itching to walk back up the railway line to just beyond King's Cross where he had seen a patch of meadowsweet under attack by black aphids. 'Never seen blackfly go for it before,' he said. 'It could be a newcomer to Britain. I'll investigate. That's the great thing about Nature – always surprises.' Ted Ellis mused about being on the other side of the fence from a local newspaper when it covered a plan to build a sewage works on an unspoilt wood he owned. His explanation of the threat to the rare fungus *Agaricus vinoso brunneus* appeared under the brutal headline 'Mushrooms – or People?'

Shortly before the gathering, the paper showed further evidence of its hierarchy's interest in the countryside, by running an article on snail-collecting in France by Richard Scott. This was the boy who had clung to the capsized hull of the family's yacht on Windermere in 1932 when his father Ted, the *Guardian*'s editor, drowned. Richard had become a distinguished foreign correspondent for the paper and his snail piece was full of zest. 'Hunting them is, surprisingly, just as exhilarating and satisfying as any other form of chase,' he wrote, in the tradition of George Muller out with the Blencathra foothounds. 'Partly it is the sheer joy of collecting anything useful or beautiful but there is also the anticipated pleasure of the eating as well as the satisfying sense of getting something for nothing, especially in France where snails cost as much as prime beef.'

If both a member of the *Guardian*'s most respected family and the editor were so enthusiastic about Country Diary matters, the column seemed in safe hands. Perhaps in gratitude, Bill Campbell sent in a diary which began, 'One of the least noticed phenomena of Spring is the appearance of the Roman snail out and about after its

*A ghost at the feast: Willam Condry was airbrushed out of this photograph of the diarists'
1974 lunch when the* Guardian *needed a 'head-and-shoulders' of Lance Samuels (extreme left)
for his obituary in 1992. The others (L to R) are Colin Luckhurst, Alistair Hetherington the*
Guardian's *editor, Enid Wilson, Ted Ellis, Henry Tegner and Harry Griffin*

long period of hibernation.' This is *Helix pomatia*, which is known as
'wallfruit' in the West Country because like Richard Scott's escargots
it makes a good meal. The column was also settling comfortably into
the new routines established by Peter Preston, who became editor
the year after the diarists' London lunch when Hetherington ended
nearly two decades at the helm.

Preston was convinced that the Country Diary would 'run itself',
as he put it to one of his Letters Editors, who now took charge of
dealing with the column along with the weather and similar small,
regular features. He was right. The principal task for the man or
woman in charge was finding enough people to fill the space, as
contributors retired, moved house or died in harness. It was never
very difficult. Dozens of would-be diarists wrote in with specimen

entries and successive editors such as Tim Radford, Patrick Ensor, Chris Maclean and Jeannette Page all remember how immediately clear it was which ones would make the grade. The method of entry was not new, as Enid Wilson's demure approach in 1950 showed, but it increasingly replaced the system of recommendation by predecessors which had led to most appointments in the past. It was more in line with recruiting competitively and on a 'level playing field', which was becoming standard practice, and ultimately a legal requirement.

The other change, as the decade gave way to the 1980s, was a deliberate increase in the diarists' numbers and an attempt to fill the gaps in their coverage of the country. Chris Maclean, an unmistakable Scot, recruited Ray Collier from his native patch and also made the first overseas step by picking a retired schoolteacher, Sarah Poyntz, to send diaries from Ireland, where she lives in the limestone landscape of the Burren. Other contributors helped to widen the coverage by their own moves, notably Colin Luckhurst whose 42 years have spanned the Shetland Isles, Lincolnshire, Peeblesshire, Edinburgh, West Cornwall, Bristol, Gloucestershire and now, in retirement, Brittany. They were encouraged, too, to report more from their holidays overseas, which, in tune with the times, were increasingly far-flung. Bulletins followed from France, central Europe and North Africa – although not always without stress. Harry Griffin's daughter Sandra still winces when she recalls how her father's meticulous arrangements with Kendal post office were replicated during skiing holidays in the Rockies, at the expense of family calm.

Cockles and muscle
❧ JANUARY 1973 ☙

From time to time nature conservationists suffer major defeats. A few years ago we lost the battle of Cow Green and so a part of

Upper Teesdale, in county Durham, with its botanical treasures, was flooded. This winter in Wales we have lost the battle of Burry Inlet and thousands of oystercatchers have been shot by permission of the Secretary of State for Wales and the Minister of Agriculture. Why? Because the birds are allegedly reducing the number of cockles in an area where cockling is a local industry. But if the cockles have declined, what proof is there that oystercatchers are responsible? It could be pollution of the water by the local tinplate factories. More likely it is because the cockles are being overfished by man, just as whales are. There is another point. Even if oystercatchers are reducing the cockle population, will this shooting produce any reduction of oystercatchers in Burry Inlet? Will not their place be taken immediately by oystercatchers from less favourable feeding grounds? Who better than the Ministry of Agriculture to know that the shooting of woodpigeons is a futile exercise? In pre-myxomatosis Pembrokeshire millions of rabbits were trapped every year. But this only encouraged the rest to breed more enthusiastically to keep the numbers up. Surely it should have been proved conclusively that oystercatchers were responsible for a reduction in cockles before these horrible and probably futile killings were allowed. Whatever happened to British justice?

William Condry

Merciful mowers
ꙮ AUGUST 1973 ꙮ

The mowing of road verges by lengthsmen has been discontinued in this county and the work is now undertaken by a smaller labour force equipped with mechanical mowers and hedge-trimmers capable of doing the work much more swiftly and economically. There are critics of the new method who deplore the ruthlessness of the machines and point out that whereas the countrymen who kept the roadsides tidy in the old days would often spare a bird's nest discovered in the long grass, such things go by the board in the new regime. However, a degree of humanity does enter into the planning of these operations. There is an early cut carried out in June and this is confined to the few feet of fairly level verge next to roads where only an occasional ground-nester chooses to set up house. The second trimming, which involves a broader sweep to include the overhang of hedges, takes place between late July and September when the risk to birds is slight. So far as the plant life of waysides is concerned I have noticed a tendency for cow parsley and hogweed to flourish more than ever, probably because these biennials flower relatively early and are able to shed seed before the second cut takes place, while their seedlings also enjoy the benefit of free access to light which results from the close double trim. Many perennial plants also cope quite well and although they are cut back in late summer, most of them, such as the knapweeds, field scabious and yellow toadflax, sprout and flower again in the autumn. A few late-flowering perennials, notably burdocks and mulleins, are becoming scarcer under the new regime, because all too often they are cut off in their prime and are unable to make much of a late flowering effort; but happily the highway authorities of Norfolk do have some regard to the sparing of rare and interesting flowers and make provision for special treatment when needs are made known to them.

Ted Ellis

Glimpsed from the train
❧ MAY 1974 ❧

What a tantalising experience is a long journey by express train. The route from Wilmslow to Euston passes through some lovely and unspoiled countryside and seems to be much closer to it than one is by road, but the speed of the train is such that one has only fleeting glimpses of birds and plants, some of them only half-identified before they are whisked away leaving only half-seen impressions on one's eyes. The feature of the journey which always strikes me most forcibly is the abundance of water all along the route, for one is scarcely ever out of sight of some river, canal or pool and a foreigner might be forgiven for assuming that the mute swan is the commonest as well as the most noticeable British bird. Railway embankments and cuttings are well known to be man-made nature reserves and the abundance of cowslips, at frequent intervals along the southern half of the run, emphasises this, for the cowslip has become rare nowadays as a meadow plant. The buzzard is a scarce bird on the Cheshire plain, where it breeds sporadically if at all, so that it was pleasant to watch one circling high over Wilmslow.

L.P. Samuels

By the light of the glow-worm
AUGUST 1974

'Anon it grew dark, and as it grew dark we had the pleasure to see several glow-worms.' Thus wrote Pepys about 300 years ago. Whether these luminous beetles still give pleasure to the late night traveller between Epsom and London I do not know, but certainly in my own area nowadays the pleasure is equally thrilling even if only a single insect is encountered. Before the general diminution of many species of once common insects which began somewhere around the early sixties, downland trackways above my former Berkshire home were lit by the fascinating greenish blue pinpoints of light at frequent intervals, and I often brought a specimen home and placed it in a position where we could experience Samuel Pepys' simple pleasure from the bedroom window. (Conservationists might frown on such interference, but such was the abundance in those good old days that invariably, within a day or so, a winged male was found attached to the female, and so the function of the mysterious cold light was fulfilled.) Recently a friend informed me that she had seen one glowing on the grass verge just by our railway station, but somehow the occurrence slipped her mind, and she did not tell me until a week had elapsed. I went straight to the site as soon as it was sufficiently dark, and was disappointed to find that the grass had been mown. But from beneath one swath of hay the old familiar light shone out brightly. Fearing that the grass would prob-ably be raked up and burnt, I decided to transfer this specimen to safer quarters. On the way home, in spite of the late hour, I decided to give some kindred spirits a treat and tapped on their window. It says a great deal both for the sort of friends I have and for the fasci-nation of the glow-worm that, although aroused from bed and bath respectively, the silent answer to the query 'Who's there?' – the illumination of my face by the glow-worm light – was received with delight.

W.D. Campbell

The bobbin-maker

❧ FEBRUARY 1975 ☙

There was very little sound in the valley bottom today – no wind at all – but the mistle thrushes sang loudly from the budded elms and the sound of water is seldom stilled in any Lake District valley. It is a constant background to life and once, not only a background but a necessity, for it supplied the power for many mills – bobbin, cotton and corn-mills, saw-mills and woollen mills as well as forges – so it seemed right today that as the old bobbin-maker talked of the past his voice was accompanied by the rush of water outside his cottage. He will be 90 this summer and was born in Preston where he began his working life in a big mill employing 900 men which made bobbins for India as well as for Lancashire. Then, for a short time he worked in a very small mill with a dozen men making sycamore rollers for mangles, oak bosses for cartwheels and bowling woods of lignum vitae. He moved north to this district 70 years ago to another bobbin mill using sycamore, ash, birch and beech for a variety of reels and bobbins varying in size from small cotton reels to foot-tall ones for rope. One of the rope bobbins stood beside him as he talked; it was turned by hand by a father and son who always worked together. He spoke about how the wood was blocked, sent to the kilns to dry, and fetched back for finishing, colouring and maybe waxing, and as his gentle voice flowed on his eyes smiled and his hands and one foot moved to illustrate the process – a little stamp of the foot, a twist and a lift of the hand – ghosts of a skill now almost gone from Cumbria.

Enid Wilson

Harvest of reeds
❧ MARCH 1975 ☙

Norfolk people take a great pride in their reeds which grow and ripen in golden profusion round the Broads. Just now, the winter harvest of the reed cutters is nearing its end. Sometimes the canes are grasped and severed with a sickle, like the corn of long ago; or, where the footing is firm, cutting is done with scythes fitted with a loped wand of hazel (called a 'bile') to clear the swathes; but on some of the larger sweeps of marshland mechanical cutters are used nowadays. Where the waters are a little brackish nearest the sea, the reeds are slender and their stems toughened by much silica; in the bays of broads enriched by nitrogenous pollution they grow tall and thick and look almost like bamboos. All types have their uses for the thatcher: he likes them short and thin for close packing, while long ones are useful for bonding and overlaps. Norfolk reed is in great demand, not only to satisfy traditional needs in East Anglia, but over a much wider field where it replaces the long thatching straw which is no longer available from farmland. When I visit friends in the Vale of Pewsey in Wiltshire I look with special pleasure at their house, snugly thatched against a wooded hillside, because I saw those reeds growing in sturdy ranks on my own marshes, watched them being harvested the old-fashioned way, stacked on the riverside, transported in flat-bottomed craft to a hard staithe, hand-trimmed and bunched, and finally loaded almost haystack high on trucks which took them by road to Wiltshire, where local craftsmen wove them into the crowning glory of a house.

Ted Ellis

The holly and the ivy
January 1976

As the year turns, holly berries are usually ripe but on this occasion very few local trees have any berries. As a substitute, florists have been incorporating the green berries of ivy, sprayed red, in holly wreaths, indicating, presumably, that the scarcity is not confined to my immediate neighbourhood. Ivy is in flower in the early winter and produces berries which darken in colour during the early months of the new year. It makes up for the lack of bright colour by having an intense fragrance to which insects are attracted. Ten species of butterfly and moths are thought to be dependent on the plant as a food source; flies and wasps effect its pollination. For many centuries ivy has been regarded as rather special. It received recognition in both Egyptian and Greek mythology. The origins of the English carol 'The Holly and the Ivy' go back 300 years. The 'armed and varnished' foliage of the holly offers protection to roosting birds and it is from the vicinity of a holly, situated near a street light, that another seasonal symbol, a robin, has attracted special attention to itself through outbursts of song. That in itself would

A COUNTRY DIARY

LAKE DISTRICT : There was very little sound in the valley bottom today—no wind at all—but the mistle thrushes sang loudly from the budded elms and the sound of water is seldom stilled in any Lake District valley. It is a constant background to life and, once, not only a background but a necessity for it supplied the power for the many mills—bobbin, cotton and corn-mills, saw-mills and woollen mills as well as forges — so it seemed right today that as the old bobbin maker talked of the past his voice was accompanied by the rush of water outside his cottage. He will be 90 this summer and was born in Preston where he began his working life in a big mill employing 900 men which made bobbins for India as well as for Lancashire. Then, for a short time he worked in a very small mill with a dozen men making sycamore rollers for mangles, oak bosses for cartwheels and bowling woods of lignum vitae. He moved North to this district 70 years ago to another bobbin mill using sycamore, ash, birch and beech for a variety of reels and bobbins varying in size from small cotton reels to foot-tall ones for rope. One of the rope bobbins stood beside him as he talked ; it was turned by hand by a father and son who always worked together. He spoke about how the wood was blocked, sent to the kilns to dry, and fetched back for finishing, colouring and maybe waxing and as his gentle voice flowed on his eyes smiled and his hands and one foot moved to illustrate the process—a little stamp of the foot, a twist and a lift of the hands— ghosts of a skill now almost gone from Cumbria.

ENID J. WILSON.

The diary's familiar style on the leader page for
30 years after the Second World War

not, of course, be unusual, but the song has in actual fact been heard between midnight and two o'clock, being repeated, with pauses, several times on each occasion. Robins do, indeed, sometimes sing at night, but I have not heard one singing at night at this time of year before. Perhaps some human influence can be detected in the incident for once, when the street lighting system obeyed the automatic timer and the lights went out, the plaintive song was heard no more.

Brian Chugg

The woodlouse question
❧ JUNE 1977 ❧

I mentioned woodlice in my last Diary – do they or do they not roll up when touched? It seemed a simple enough query but I could find none in my garden who rolled and quite a lot of stories and theories have unfurled (or un-rolled) since then. Readers up and down the country from near the Border to the south coast all have, it seems, their own ideas and observations gained while gardening, weeding onions, turning over leaves or simply recalling things they have heard or read. Books are not very specific. I have an old one which describes 'these funny little creatures in our gardens', calls them crustaceans and speaks of the Giant Wood Louse (sadly not saying how big 'Giant' is) and asserting that neither it nor the common louse can roll up. It puts beside them the pill beetles and pill millipedes which can and do. Another treasured gardening book is very hot on the subject. It calls them 'one of the gardener's worst foes', the damage done to costly maidenhair ferns in glass houses is especially bad for the little beasts 'gnaw away secretly at the roots' and even eat seedlings when they are barely above ground. It recommends that they are searched for each morning and killed by dousing with boiling water. I can remember seeing gardeners, when I was a child, putting grass-stuffed pots on stakes in their dahlias to trap lice and earwigs – but they were just firmly trodden on. Pill beetles must be much more benign – a reader from Buckingham calls them 'cheese beetles' because of their likeness to cheeses when rolled and a friend of hers possesses a book by the Reverend J.G. Wood (1859) who states that pill beetles were 'formerly used in medicine', being swallowed as a pill in the rolled-up state. 'I have seen a drawer of them,' he says, 'half-full of these creatures all rolled-up and ready to be swallowed.' I have (so far as I know) no complaint which necessitates rolled beetles – so there is much to be thankful for.

Enid Wilson

A bloody conundrum
❧ AUGUST 1977 ❧

The rabbit, a young buck, still warm and limp, was placed reverently in my hands by our teenage son whose first hunting triumph it was. Flushed with excitement, both at the pleasure of dropping the beast with a .22 air rifle and with the nervous release of being responsible for its death, he had reason to expect that I could deploy my amateur butcher skills and prepare the carcase for the deep freeze. After all, I can manage brown trout from the river easily enough, but then the basic anatomy of the brown trout is relatively simple when you compare it with the furry cadaver of a still warm rabbit. I considered the problem as the buck gently leaked its life blood away on a sheet of newspaper. Folk memories of skinning rabbits whole flooded through my mind but did not help with an understanding of where to make the necessary cuts. The furry skin of the beast seemed awfully tough and thick and did I really have a sharp enough knife? As the shadows of a summer evening lengthened across the garden table the problem seemed to grow more and more unsavoury. If I removed the head and skin there was still the disembowelling and removal of guts. I went inside for a drink and my wife, who I believed had the anatomical knowledge to give me the necessary advice, made it clear that it was not her scene either. I am rather relieved to notice through the window that Arthur, the domestic cat who has no scruples about taking warm mammals apart and is especially fond of young rabbits, is staggering across the garden with the buck held

163

awkwardly between his teeth. I really didn't have the energy to get up and pursue him. But in these days of pre-packed meat, how I felt I had failed in a paternal duty as I buried what Arthur left in the rhubarb patch next morning.

Colin Luckhurst

Riddle of the sands
❧ APRIL 1978 ☙

It is an accepted belief that our sand dunes, especially the oldest ones, are a product of the Middle Ages when, so the theory goes, the weather became much stormier and produced gales which quickly piled up the extensive dunes we know today. The evidence for this in Wales comes from both pre-history and history. In modern times along the Glamorgan coast, when gales have scoured away the sand down to the original soil level, quite a number of prehistoric artefacts have been revealed. There also a mediaeval settlement is reputed to have been overwhelmed by sand. Similarly at Newborough dunes in Anglesey, a tradition has come down of a village of the Middle Ages being abandoned as the sand advanced and smothered it. Such legends are an enjoyable part of our folk-lore but they take on an extra dimension if someone stumbles on evidence which shows them to be true. This has happened at the now pine-covered Newborough dunes and I was happy this week to join a party of students from Salford University when, under the guidance of the Forestry Commission, we were shown the substantial remains of a cottage recently excavated out of a sand dune. It was quite moving to see these long-buried walls and to speculate on their age. And also to sense that many more such buildings, each with its story to tell, probably lie beneath the sands all around.

William Condry

A bizarre wooden beast

ᎧᏋ MAY 1979 ᎧᏋ

Should you be travelling in Kent at the time of the May festivities do not be alarmed if you encounter the most remarkable of its mediaeval mysteries, the Hooden Horse. In the eastern half of the county near the original landing place of the Germanic invaders, Woden was especially powerful, leaving his pagan presence in village names. He also left his horse, a bizarre wooden beast, a large head on a long pole, possibly a relic of the early Teuton sacrifice of the horse at the winter solstice. Now the beast makes its appearance at other times of the rural year, including the spring festival, garlanded with flowers, bedecked with ribbons and accompanied by hand bells. According to local experts the horse sometimes assumes female guise, adopting names like Mollie or The Old Woman, so the Hooden Horse gets mixed up with witches and broomsticks, a confusion of image typical of folklore. The most conspicuous feature of the horse is its mouth which clanks open and shut with ferocious intent, the teeth being made with large hobnails, giving it another local name of Hob the Nob and another link in the ritual chain with the hobby horse. Interpretations flourish with every festive brew, especially along the banks of the Stour where an inn proudly bears the Hooden emblem. As the horse clanks in procession it seems that Hengist and Horsa have only just landed and the invasion of the old gods is imminent. Its intent now is purely one of goodwill though it reputedly frightened one lady to death and drove another from her invalid chair, cured by panic. Today it seems as innocent as the Morris Men and children who dance in its wake.

John T. White

Food for fungi
❧ NOVEMBER 1980 ☙

Early in January 1976, a great gale swept East Anglia, bringing down thousands of trees. In my own woods hurricane gusts felled a hundred oaks in less than an hour, together with some noble beeches and numerous shallow-rooted silver birches. Since then, many of the trunks have remained undisturbed, some overgrown with brambles, honeysuckles and bracken. Within a short time, certain fungi began to sprout from beneath the bark, notably crinkled, gelatinous cup-fungi and leathery, bracket-forming stereums, while olive-black bulgarias adorned the oaks in profusion. In due course these pioneers were joined and eventually supplanted by other fungi. In summer the timber tended to dry out to some extent and fungal growth was arrested, but with the return of moister conditions in autumn and winter attacks were renewed and the work of gradually reducing the trees to touchwood and, ultimately, humus, made further progress. The smaller twigs and branches have by now largely crumbled and fallen away, macerated finally by the nibblings of mites, insects, and woodlice; but the trunks continue to be embellished with clusters of yellow, brown and white toadstools, waxy orange frills of phlebias, woody, vari-coloured brackets and swarms of smaller members of the fraternity. Occasionally flushes of living protoplasm emerge. It is fascinating to follow the procession of strange and beautiful organisms carrying out their long-established function of clearing forests of their fallen giants. And just as lions, vultures, jackals and lesser fry follow one another in demolishing fallen beasts, there is an order of priority among the scavengers. Only now, more than four years after my oaks met with disaster, am I finding for the first time an elegant apricot-gilled, olive-topped agaric (*Pahellus serotinus*) sprouting from them.

Ted Ellis

Clamour of the lambs

❧ MAY 1981 ❧

The great bowl of the dale was filled with noise – the pleasant, homely noise of hundreds of sheep and their newly born lambs. First, perhaps, a deep-throated 'baa' from close at hand, answered by a plaintive note in a higher key, from across the intake fields, and then a few rather mournful chords, a peremptory command to her offspring from some impatient, old ewe and, all the time, a high-pitched bleating from the lambs. As the evening shadows crept across the lovely, green turf the clamour grew more insistent and the lambs became more frisky – enjoying their last hour before sleep, just like youngsters, with games on the grass and 'follow my leader' through the gap in the old stone wall. With enviable energy the little, clumsy bundles of wool fought and jostled one another, sometimes struggling for possession of a little mound of turf or trying out the new-found springs in their wobbly legs with high jumps and somersaults. Meanwhile, the ewes stolidly cropped the turf, keeping an eye on their excited charges and now and again replying to a frightened bleat with a reassuring grumble. Something like 200,000 of these cuddlesome creatures will have been born this spring in central Lakeland when lambing time is over – all of them unrecognisable from their fellows by you or me but immediately identifiable by their proud mothers and even, in many cases, by the farmers. Here is the biggest and most important crop in the country – thousands of baby Herdwicks, Swaledales, Roughs and crosses, the first-named 'heafed' to the same stretch of fellside that their ancestors have occupied for generations.

Harry Griffin

The story of a field
❧ JULY 1981 ❧

This could be called the history of a field, perhaps of many fields now, but this one is on a valley slope edged by trees on three sides. Fifty years ago it had a lodge at one corner and a well-kept drive to a fine house. It was only grazed periodically. The turf had moonwort and adders' tongues in spring; in summer there were orchids – twayblade, fragrant and butterfly ones – and, in autumn, betony and scabious, all good for moths and butterflies. There were mushrooms too. Then the estate was broken up and timber was felled in a wood and dragged out smashing many field drains so that springs broke out in the grass. Gorse and briars grew on the drive but still tree pipits sang and nested at its top. In latter years, however, it had too many sheep and horses with foals and the land grew poorer, but the ultimate disaster was ponies. They churned up the wet ground with their hooves, chewed the hedges and tore up even its coarse grass in winter. Then they were given hay balls which fetched sorrel and docks. But this spring they were banished and the land was fed. Today I was asked back to see it again and, suddenly, time was turned back. The adders' tongues and moonwort have gone, perhaps for ever, but there are orchids – twayblade, a few spotted and armies of butterfly ones, greeny-white and sweet to smell. Dusky chimney-sweep moths hovered over the tall grass and a fat orange underwing was in its roots. I am told that there may be cows one day soon but perhaps some at least of the flowers will stay.

Enid Wilson

Private Keep Out
❧ AUGUST 1981 ❧

I made the mistake of looking at the mansion set back in Kentish parkland too long and too intently. When I completed my stroll down the footpath to the moated site I wanted to see, I was quickly surrounded by an impressive band, like something out of a film about the French Foreign Legion. I just had time to note that the moated farm now bore the device of a long-horned cow and a name that originated at least 2,000 miles from Kent. Why was I photographing their house? I had no camera but my binoculars, which are unusually small and better-suited to the front row of the stalls than distant landscapes, excited them. I was obviously up to no good. Somehow I felt that my explanation of mediaeval colonising patterns in the Low Weald and the significance of moated sites in the thirteenth century did not interest them. When I was accused of walking over their land, I was provoked into a short but pertinent lecture on rights-of-way in general and that particular right-of-way especially as an ancient drove road. I pointed to the long-horned cows to emphasise the point. Cattle drives, in Kent? They looked incredulous. The shotgun one of them waved about may have been pointing out the more notable features of the landscape but I doubted it and got even more British, talking about the Queen's highway. After all, I was standing on the road at the time. Then came the unanswerable question. Why was I walking? I looked down at my boots, my grubby trousers, and the rest of my paraphernalia, felt the sweat on my brow from the exertions of a summer day, and knew that there was no answer they would understand. The culture gap was too wide even for the delights of the Weald to bridge. I had to leave them to their misgivings.

John T. White

The death of the elms
❧ JULY 1982 ☙

In the hedges in my immediate vicinity considerable patches of elm – suckers – still survive, and recently, in a plantation of mainly young beech in our local forest, I was gratified to find that during current clearing of the undergrowth, apparently healthy elm saplings which had not been planted had been left unscathed. But so far I have not come across a single mature elm which escaped the ravages of the disease which has drastically altered our landscape during the last decade. But a few miles away, just over the Gloucestershire border, a correspondent informs me that recently he was delighted to find two splendid specimens of elm, about 60 feet high, still flourishing. He sent me a leaf, which, tentatively, I have identified as that of the Huntington elm, a chance hybrid which originated as a nursery seedling over two centuries ago and thereafter was planted extensively for its ornamental value. Since, according to Alan Mitchell's league table of outstanding specimens, a Gloucestershire tree is (or was?) the finest known example of this form, it seems likely that these survivors, growing in isolation from any other elms in a Cotswold village, are of the same ancestry. In view of their apparent immunity, it is interesting to note that, just over 40 years ago, Dutch arboriculturalists raised what were then hailed as immune varieties from this same strain, but, alas, even these proved susceptible to the more virulent form of Dutch elm disease which struck some thirty years later. An ominous aside in my correspondent's letter is: 'I did just notice a very small branch dead at the top of one tree.'

W.D. Campbell

Excuse me, I've lost my girlfriend
NOVEMBER 1982

A round of the Langdale fells, starting with Jack's Rake on Pavey Ark and finishing with the descent of Hell Gill, was enlivened by a curious encounter on Hanging Knotts. The day, for a change, had been clear with gusty winds on the tops but, after an interesting scramble through the crags above Rossett Gill, I emerged into thick cloud on the stormy plateau, quite close to Ore Gap. Almost at once I met another lone walker, picking his way in the direction of Esk Pike but, as he explained, hopelessly lost. Could I help, he asked. He had left his girlfriend below in the mist, after walking along something called The Belt, and had been trying to find her for the last hour without success. No, he had no compass. 'Could it have been The Band?' I asked and he thought that might have been the name, so I had to tell him that he was about a mile out of his way and going in the opposite direction. With obvious relief, he agreed to accompany me over Bowfell and eventually, some distance above Three Tarns, we found his companion who seemed to have weathered the wait with fortitude, despite the cold. There was a touching reunion. This young man was not the first to go astray in mist on the extensive Bowfell summit plateau – or in many places in the Lakeland fells in poor conditions. One wonders, indeed, how many casual walkers in the hills carry compasses and know how to use them. Accurate compass work is the most satisfying reward of a day in the clouds and a very necessary insurance. If regularly taught in schools compass navigation could save lives, avoid distress – and provide fun. And, despite reports to the contrary, compasses do work accurately on Bowfell – provided they are held in the hand and not placed, in certain places only, on the rock.

Harry Griffin

Supermouse

April 1983

At last a day of real warmth, the path through the hanger wood sunlit and dry. A time for just standing and staring and it was my good fortune that I did so, otherwise I should have missed a vignette of woodland life that would not have been out of place in a comic cartoon. A ripple running through the leaf litter turned out to be a weasel in hot pursuit of a wood mouse. The mouse ran or, rather, bounced in a succession of small leaps, clearing the ground flora like a hurdler. The weasel was gaining and they tangled together by the roots of an old beech tree. I assumed that was the end of the mouse, but the quarry proved very elusive and in the chase that followed even had the temerity to jump over the weasel. There was no paralysis of fear in this hunt. If anything, fear drove the mouse to even greater agility. At one point it crossed the path I was standing on, long tail outstretched, long, pointed ears in a high state of alertness. Then, unbelievably, it met the weasel again and the two ran past each other just like characters from a comic strip. The weasel turned sharply in its tracks, but too late. The mouse was away to some underground haven. The weasel, baffled, took up its stance on a large stone and raised its nine-inch body to the full extent to gain the maximum view of its hunting territory. Finding nothing in sight, it roamed back towards the beech tree, dived into the leaf litter and disturbed two more wood mice and they, too, raced away to different points of the compass in very swift and straight lines. The weasel lost them, too. Supposedly one of the more efficient killers of the woodland underworld and small enough to follow mice along their runs, the weasel hunts by day and night, especially with a young litter to feed. I have seen many a weasel out on patrol but never a display like this.

John T. White

Night owl

❧ OCTOBER 1984 ❧

It was an ordinary autumn day, one of cloud and sun. But after noon the warmth got the better of the mist. Bumblebees and Red Admiral butterflies came to feed on the pale mounds of heath bloom beside the bird-bath, but the butterflies stayed on to bask half-asleep in the warmth. Tonight is not ordinary at all: a strange night with another dimension, one to remember. The brown owls have come right up to the wide open, curtained window and are probably in the tall birch tree just outside. I shall not stir the curtain. Perhaps it is an owl family for their range of sound covers everything from confiding chirrups to a full owl cry. My cat is out, too, and I cannot help but wonder where he is and what part he has in the night. He also is a silent hunter, can turn his head almost full circle and sits, cock-eared to the mice below the sill. His eyes, large and full-orbed, can fix; more 'owl' than 'cat', indeed an owl without wings. The sky was barred with cloud again at sunset but now it is clear and cold, almost a frosty sky with only a half-moon and glittering stars which snap as they do in real frost. The bats were here at dusk for the first time for months, hunting assiduously round the outlines of the spruce spires. Perhaps they too are laying up reserves for the cold to come? Yes, so long as the owl does not 'call my name' it will be a night to remember . . . but not for the mice with bats, cats, and owls seeming to conspire against them.

Enid Wilson

CHAPTER NINE

When Things Go Wrong

Many things can happen to a Country Diary between the writer's desk and the *Guardian*'s sub-editors, and they do. But in the late 1980s the spate of glitches had a happy result, when a printer on the paper called Peter Postance joined the diary team. It was in the aftermath of the war of Wapping, when Rupert Murdoch closed *The Times* for a year and survived street battles to introduce new technology and break the power of the printing unions. Change duly followed at the *Guardian*, more amicably. After a symbolic funeral for hot-metal printing, when a coffin was 'hammered out' in the composing room at Farringdon Road in the way that printers traditionally were on their retirement, ten 'comps' were recruited to work alongside journalists as 'systems operators' of the new, often baffling processes.

Peter was one of them, and two nights before Christmas 1989 he noticed that Jeannette Page, who edited the Country Diary as well as readers' letters and various other sections, was looking anxious. He went over and learnt that the diary had not arrived or was lost or possibly – in those early electronic days – unintentionally deleted. Their conversation turned briefly to Peter's weekend fishing and how he'd watched a baby water rat being savaged by a mink ('Evil creatures – let loose by the animal liberation people probably,' he still recalls). 'Peter,' appealed Jeannette, 'you couldn't do me sixty lines on that as a diary, could you? Now?' Postance did, showing the draft to another sub-editor friend Des Christie ('I didn't want to make myself look a complete twat'). The result not only passed muster but prompted the then features editor Alan Rusbridger to ask Postance for more. They were used as first reserves and as a result, says Peter, 'sometimes waited patiently in the system for weeks – they often had to be adjusted at the last minute as the seasons and weather had changed in the meantime'.

Rusbridger, like Alistair Hetherington, had a long-standing interest in the diary and enjoyed suggesting other occasional innovations. Soon after the Postance episode, the writer and beer specialist Richard Boston came into the office full of excitement about an incident involving his sister, their father and an eel. 'Alan just said two words to me,' he recalls: 'Country Diary.' Thus Boston made his solitary excursion onto the diary patch, an entry with another point of interest. It is much the longest in this collection, inadvertently highlighting the skill at précis of the regulars. Another one-off diarist, Jack Abbott, was the stepfather of Geraldine Petley, PA to another *Guardian* journalist, Richard Gott.

This on-the-run style of editing could work both ways, and the Country Diary files are full of yelps from contributors at the cavalier way their careful paragraphs were treated. Early evening at a national newspaper in the days of hot metal was no place for the faint-hearted, and subbing shifts might also be in the hands of casuals, to whom names such as Bill Campbell or Brian Chugg meant nothing. Some of the fiercest complaints on record are from Harry Griffin (Lieut.-Colonel retired), who meticulously cut his typewriter paper so that the last line would meet the stipulated length. In the hurly-burly of breaking news, prima donna political commentators and leaders which could not be cut, there was in practice no such thing as stipulated length. As a journalist Harry knew this, but his patience was taxed by the occasional complete disappearance of his piece or alternatively its use two days running. The much more mild-mannered Enid Wilson could also be goaded beyond endurance. After five of her diaries in a row in 1971 had misprints or mis-spellings, she wrote to Hetherington to say: 'I am not an awkward person, but I have had complaints from a lot of people, from the local postman to an ex-librarian of Edinburgh university. I am sur-prised how many people seem to read it.'

The paper, to its credit, didn't try to brush off these grumbles. When Patrick Ensor was in charge, he responded to a Griffin salvo with a reassurance which put the diarist on a par with one of the most famous *Guardian* journalists of the time. 'I share your horror at the way your very fine piece of writing was cut, and I have written a hard-hitting memo to all those who do the page in my absence not to repeat such brutality. There was no reason why James Cameron's piece could not have been trimmed back to accommodate your Country Diary. Please do not contemplate resigning; you are one of our most highly-appreciated diarists, which makes Sunday night's savagery even more hurtful.' When Bill Campbell suffered the galling experience of having a diary 'livened up' by a sub-editor, he was allowed to put things right the following week. His diary in June 1986 concluded: 'PS. It came as a surprise to me to read in my last Country Diary that the fox was "furiously feeding" on the lambs' tails; what I wrote merely stated that it was "very actively engaged in finding food".' Tough Fleet Street journalists perhaps had a soft spot for the Country Diarists because most were so modest. Janet Case reacted typically when she was recruited in 1925 on the recommen-dation of Helena Swanwick. She havered and wavered, writing to C.P. Scott that she felt terribly diffident and worried that she had been too hasty in accepting his 10/6 a week (£25 today). A weekend spent with Mrs Swanwick bucked her up.

Fault could of course lie on the diarists' side. The introduction of the *Guardian*'s Corrections and Clarifications column in 1997 saw the Country Diary as well represented in the blunder box as any other section of the paper. And sometimes there were graver errors. One contributor was reprimanded after the editor of a farming magazine pointed out an uncanny resemblance between a Country Diary and a light-hearted editorial of his own. The diarist apologised and fortunately the victim took it in good part. 'To tell you the truth I'm rather flattered,' he wrote to the *Guardian*'s managing editor. 'But if it happens again, I could perhaps be paid half the contributor's cheque. I realise this will be a paltry sum of course, but as you are no doubt aware, farming is under increasing pressure these days . . . and every little helps.'

Simply getting the diary to the paper was also a strain on occasions. In the earliest days, C.P. Scott showed a mistrust of the post familiar today when he asked Coward, de Selincourt and Swanwick to mail their pieces two days in advance, rather than the day before. Harry Griffin always superstitiously used the main post office in Kendal and always posted the little envelope himself. By the 1970s, the London editors were regularly appealing for diarists to phone their paragraphs direct to the telephone copytakers, but this could be intimidating. Any reporter of that era recalls copytakers' mischievous interruptions such as 'Is there much more of this?' or 'Are you on the staff?' When you were writing about great crested grebes, it was all the more challenging. But diarists won over even these world-weary, heard-it-all-before colleagues. William Condry remembered dictating on a crackly line and finding that 'although occasionally the spelling of Welsh place-names defeats the copy-typists, I have never ceased to wonder at their skill and speed; and sometimes they have entered into the spirit of the moment and offered approving comments, or even suggested a better word here and there'. There is a direct line from his comments to Thomas Coward's respect for amateur village naturalists.

The diary team continued to expand in the 1980s and early 1990s, supplemented by other *Guardian* journalists with features and ever-increasing news and background coverage of environmental, wildlife and countryside affairs. The paper's old spirit continued in articles such as a dramatic report on winter lambing in the Yorkshire Dales by Geoffrey Taylor, who managed to combine his associate editorship and leader-writing duties with running the post office in the remote hamlet of Litton ('via Skipton', as his official address put it). But Peter Preston and lieutenants like Rusbridger were having to keep up with competition by creating a new *Guardian*, far larger than the 20-page issues at the height of C.P. Scott's glory. Environmental matters had a whole section to themselves. In this context the Country Diary, unchanged for decades at between 250 and 350 words, was pro rata a fraction of its earlier size; to keep up, it theoretically deserved half a page. The proof of its lasting value was that, miniature though it was and after the late 1980s tucked away at the back of the G2 features section, it continued to attract shoals of letters and a very high score in reader surveys.

Summoned by bells

December 1985

Sound can do strange things in quiet November weather. A thick mist along the valley can deaden everything but given a clear valley and a low cloud layer it can travel far. A friend who lived all her life on a farm near Thirlmere used to say that she could sometimes hear the bells of Crosthwaite church clearly – six miles away and in the next valley. It seems that their voices can rise, hit the cloud layer and echo southwards. The ring is an old one. In 1699 the churchwarden's accounts record four shillings and sixpence a year for the four ringers and five shillings for a new bell rope. In 1706 it was sixteen shillings with ale for Thanksgiving Days and November the Fifth. By 1714 the Great Bell needed attention so it was taken down, sent by cart to Whitehaven, and by ship to Dublin to be re-cast. Those accounts have almost forty items varying from 'one shilling the night the bell was cast' to 'one pound and sixteen for our diet, lodging and washing our linen'. The grand total – belfry to belfry – was just over £37 and the bells rang for the King's Coronation in 1715. Six bells were hung in 1775 and with that change-ringing began. A Yorkshire man arrived in Keswick with a small travelling circus and, a shoemaker by trade, he stayed on to follow it and to teach the art of change-ringing in the belfry. Ringers had discipline. A board still in the church adjures a man to have an upright heart and there are fines for wrong-doing – eightpence for ringing with spur or hat or for overturning a bell. Times and bells may have changed but most of the names of those old ringers can still be met in the flesh in a Keswick street.

Enid Wilson

A robin helps MI5
December 1986

Many of our larger birds – particularly predators, gulls, herons and rooks – eject pellets or castings of indigestible matter orally instead of through the usual alimentary tract; and, of course, since these are proportionately large, they may regularly be found. Less well-known practitioners of this technique are members of the thrush family, such as the blackbirds which are strewing my garden with small cylindrical pellets consisting of the tough skins and seeds of rose-hips. Another member of the same family, the robin, uses the same method, but its minute castings are more rarely found. Now the second example I have ever come across has provided an interesting link with the MI5 court proceedings in Australia. Many years ago, on the old BBC Third Programme, I served on a panel which included a naturalist who shared my interest in birds' pellets, and needed an example of one from a robin for his collection. A few days later my very tame household robin, which knew its way about the house, deposited a pill-like black pellet on the sheets of my turned-back bed, and this was duly sent to fill the missing gap. Now a robin has deposited a similar pellet – consisting mainly of the legs and wing-cases of small beetles – on my bird-table. Of course, my mind went back to the former occasion, and soon afterwards when reading of the complicated proceedings in Sydney, I was amazed to discover that my pellet-collecting acquaintance was mentioned: not as a naturalist, but as once head of the counter-subversion department of MI5.

W.D. Campbell

Studied by seals
June 1987

Northumberland: We are bobbing in the swell which laps the rocks of the Longstone, our coble *Glad Tidings* has dropped anchor to allow its passengers to watch the seals. The Farne Islands host thousands of these mammals and there has always been conflict with the fishermen. Billy Shiel, our helmsman, told us that the seals can be seen jumping up to catch the struggling salmon while they are being netted. On Holy Island, the net fishermen fire guns over the heads of the seals to scare them off. Feeding on their regular diet of codling we saw several large seals tossing the fish up and skinning them. Heaving themselves about on the rocks, the bulls resemble lethargic slugs but the cows and calves are more graceful and many swam quite close to our boat, curious to see us. We land on Staple Island which hosts avian high-rise flats, 11,000 pairs of guillemots nest here during the season. Shags build nests in extraordinarily precarious clefts and the warden told me that if the chicks moved even a foot from the nest, the mother wouldn't feed them. So, there is a certain amount of infant mortality. The wardens record nests, watch and count birds and, where necessary, collect gull eggs, because the gull population needs to be controlled. Gulls will kill lesser birds and eat their eggs. Last month, there was an interesting sighting of a fall of 35 bluethroats (a North European robin) which paused on the Farne Islands for several days. 'I watched them practically night and day,' the young warden said. 'It was a marvellous sighting and I know experienced ornithologists who would have given anything to have been here.'

Veronica Heath

Loveliest of trees
⟡ JUNE 1988 ⟡

I have never seen the apple blossom more lovely than it is now. Most of my remaining trees are old, over 50, and since they are grown on a dwarfing stock cannot last much longer. However, even if this should be their last spring they are seeing it out in a shine of glory, each leaf, each petal, is flying its own little flag in the face of time. Two small new trees were planted amongst them on a cold February day earlier in the year – an apple and a pear. I had the apple planted out of sheer pig-headedness for I was told it would not bear fruit in my lifetime but I shall be happy either way. I shall be pleased if it produces even one apple but I am quite content to 'wait on'. The infant apple tree has neat rosettes of blossom up each small branch but the pear – never tidy flowerers – does as it pleases. Fruit growing has altered a lot over recent years and it no longer seems to be said that you grow pears for your heirs. Apple blossom time is always a bit nostalgic for me as I have no hive bees now but I still remember all the hard work and the fun the local beekeepers had together in sunny Saturday afternoons in the summer. One picture sticks in my mind especially. It was a hot day and my husband and I had been to a school Speech Day and were to meet our fellow bee-keepers at Bassenthwaite. We had our bee hats with us so my best hat, a pretty thing, seldom worn, was parked on a hive roof to be joined by an old tweed hat and crowned with the village policeman's helmet — and very happy they looked all together and typical of any beekeeping 'do' up here. There are few bees out today but there are knots of Small White butterflies dancing over the lady's smocks (*Cardamine pratensis*), 'all silver and white' in the tall grass below the apple trees. A lovely sight but not to growers of brassicas.

Enid Wilson

A savage intruder
◆ DECEMBER 1988 ◆

While pike-fishing on a rare dry afternoon recently, we noticed a group of magpies and crows squabbling amongst bushes on the bank of the Thames. My son stopped the outboard motor and let the boat drift nearer to the cause of the disturbance. At the water's edge we were amazed to see a wild mink with a baby rat in its mouth being harangued by a parent rat and four or five assorted members of the crow family who were obviously hoping that the mink would drop the prize and take fright. Not so. The mink, having apparently dared to plunder the rats' nest while hunting, was already savouring its future supper and did not intend to give it up to a group of feathered scavengers, however insistent they were. The parent rat forgot its offspring and retreated the moment it saw us, closely followed by the crows who sat in nearby hawthorn bushes loudly protesting our interference. The mink, however, stood quite still, firmly gripping its now dead prey by the head and peering at us through black beady eyes, showing no fear whatever, even to the point of making me feel that we, ourselves, were perhaps going to be subjected to an attack.

Printer turned country diarist: Peter Postance puts his own column
'to bed' in the Guardian *composing room*

When only a metre or so separated us, the mink decided that this confrontation had gone far enough and, towing the unfortunate rat, he swam very strongly to the opposite bank where he melted into the bushes. We have never seen wild mink before in this area although there have been reported sightings on the nearby River Wey, which runs into the Thames less than a mile upstream. These descendants of escapers from mink farms are moving away from their parents to claim their own territories as they reach maturity and are spreading further and further along the rivers. The local water authorities have taken a dim view of this intrusion. So have local fishing clubs who regard the wild mink as a menace to fish and other wildlife. Local rats would probably agree with them.

Peter Postance

Dream island
SEPTEMBER 1989

As part of the Royal Society for the Protection of Birds centenary celebrations, the local members' group organised the Havergate Adventure. The island is Suffolk's loneliest nature reserve and normally attracts only a limited number of visitors. It was planned to open the island to the public for nine days, ferrying them there and giving a guided tour. The sight of 200 or so avocets feeding in the shallow water with their sweeping action, for which their curved bills are especially adapted, brought gasps of pleasure from the birdwatchers. These elegant birds overwinter at Havergate and are joined by thousands of wildfowl driven south by the arctic winter. Mallard, teal, widgeon, pintail, shelduck, tufted duck, pochard and shoveller all use the reserve as their winter quarters. Sharing the island with the wildfowl are thousands of waders, curlew, whimbrel, snipe, four types of plover – green, ringed, golden and grey – knot, ruff, turnstone, dunlin and redshank. These flocks are sometimes joined by a rarity, recently a little egret. Birds suddenly taking to the air in panic as a marsh harrier drifts overhead is a sight to be remembered, with flocks wheeling in all directions, and redshank giving a noisy alarm call. The curlew's evocative notes float across the marshes and provide music for onlookers, while a blue flash speeding past is a handsome kingfisher. Swallows nest in the hides and recently one nest was raided by a barn owl, leaving a pathetic heap of feathers on the floor. Short-eared owls are present, as are kestrels and an occasional hobby. Hares, stoats, frogs, toads and lizards are to be found and the warden has listed 137 different plants growing. Truly a dream island.

Jack Abbott

The longest diary ever
ᴥ OCTOBER 1989 ᴥ

It was not just for the sake of the rhyme that in *A Shropshire Lad* A.E. Housman called Clun the quietest place under the sun. Clun is not as quiet as it was in Housman's day because the RAF use that part of Shropshire for practising low-altitude flying in small, very fast, sinister-looking planes, prompting yet again the question of why the hell don't they leave the job to Matthias Rust who landed in Red Square in his much less expensive Cessna. Apart from the intrusions of these weapons of war, Clun is still as quiet and peaceful as I imagine it was in Housman's day, and on a visit to my father in late September there were many much more attractive identifiable flying objects. It was a delight to watch a wagtail earning its name hopping about on the gravel of the stream that flows under Clun's narrow stone bridge. Recently my father saw a full moon in broad daylight. He had been bird-watching and had his binoculars with him. He looked through them at the moon and by pure chance caught in the binoculars' field of vision an extraordinary sight. A buzzard was circling the moon. Chance seems to be generous in Clun. Walking down a hillside I caught out of the corner of my eye something unusual. In a trickle of water there was something long and shiny. An eel, nearly three foot long, pointed in a downhill direction. Alive, but looking as though it was near its last gasp. It was lying in only about a quarter of an inch of water. I'm no expert on eels, but I've heard that they can cross fields. Even so, we all agreed that this was a very thirsty eel. Presumably it came from the pond higher up the hill and had decided that now that summertime was nearly over, and this drought looked as though it would never break, it was time to up sticks (or whatever eels do) and make tracks down the hill to the river at the bottom. My sister ran to the house and came back with a bucket of water. When we had managed to get the eel into it, she headed off to the river. The hill was steep and the eel was reviving. It escaped, and lay on the ground wondering what to do next. I am terrified of anything that even resembles a snake but my father is more intrepid, and made to pick up the eel. It was immediately apparent why people say slippery as an eel. The eel was very slippery indeed. I managed to find some sack-cloth which we threw over the eel and wrapped it up. Then we (that is to say my father) carried it to the river and dropped it in. It went into an S shape and headed off with a wag of the tail which seemed to combine a thank-you with a good-bye. And so, I suppose, off to the Sargasso Sea. Good luck, Eel, with luck like yours I'm sure you'll make it.

Richard Boston

Lightning and limpets
JANUARY 1990

Christmas Eve: a thunder and lightning storm raged in the Bay. On a night with but a sliver of moon the hills, valley, the crashing waves on the Rine and the whole agitated sea to the Martello Tower on Finavarra were illuminated. Then, above the tempest noise, a loud explosion and all electricity and phone lines were cut. A lightning or thunder-bolt had hit the church. Immediately the hotel proprietor let it be known that people could cook their Christmas dinners there (this included those in the holiday cottages). However, the emergency crew had the electricity back within five hours. The phones took several days; the wires in the cables had melted and many telephones needed individual attention. How lucky we were that there were no injuries or deaths. On New Year's Day we took a walk in mild sunshine on the Flaggy Shore, the Bay pale blue, its waters barely in motion. During the first few days of January we noticed bulb-tops emerging, roses still blooming in village gardens and winter heather, pink and white in flower. Mary Ann while rebuilding one of our drystone walls found piles of limpet and winkle shells between rocks. We thought birds had left them although the shells looked very old, their surface pitted, their colours faded. On inquiring we were told that such piles of shells indicate that once there had been a house there. It would have been a house with sod walls and roof which would when vacated fall and leave no traces. Only the seashells now speak to the past. The inhabitants, especially in the last Irish Famine of the 1840s, might have survived on limpets and winkles. '. . . the pity of it,' yet Homer's 'unvintaged sea' WAS vintaged by those in such sore distress and need, sustaining them in life so that their descendants now see in this New Year.

Sarah Poyntz

Attacked by a swan
MAY 1990

A river trip to a friend's house was comically disrupted recently by a swan who decided to attack my boat. On the way to Shepperton lock weir I noticed a large cob swan swimming towards me. As he got alongside, his beak almost level with my face, he suddenly flew at me. I pushed him away with an oar, speeded up the motor and was relieved when the gap between us widened to about a hundred yards or so. However, as I slowed down he started in my direction, running across the water flapping his powerful wings. Worried that he might tip me in, I attempted to swerve out of his way but he flew into the side of the boat, his wing knocking over my bag and scattering its contents. He repeated this several times until I eventually outran him. A few hours later, on my way home, I rounded the bend near D'Oyly Carte Island and there was the swan again. I slowed down to pass him, hoping he hadn't noticed me, but to my dismay heard the familiar sound of his feet and wings slapping the surface of the water. As he drew level I splashed him vigorously with an oar, displacing gallons of water, much of it coming into the boat. Suddenly he stopped and, flapping his wings, stood upright on the water, a frightening sight close up. Then he calmly turned and swam away in the opposite direction, his honour apparently satisfied. We have had other experiences of the eccentric behaviour of these otherwise lovely birds, always at this time of the year when they are protecting their eggs or young, or when they have failed to win, or have lost, a mate. Sometimes, ironically, for reasons not altogether unconnected with us fishermen.

Peter Postance

Proud to be a husband
ᘓ SEPTEMBER 1990 ᘔ

For over thirty years I have belonged to an unofficial, exclusive male club called the WI Husbands. We are the chaps who weekly or monthly see our ladies sallying gaily off to those mysterious institute gatherings where, amid much chat and laughter, goodness knows what larks the dear things get up to. My wife's institute is in a village so small it is hard to believe that a WI branch has held together here for all of sixty-two years. Yet there are the minute books to prove it. Written in many hands and styles, they reveal a marvellous history of parish activities, for nothing much would have happened here over the years without the WI to take the lead. The chronicle reveals the ladies entertaining themselves with fun and games, keep-fit, yoga, folk dancing and coach trips to far-away places. It also shows them in earnest pursuit of knowledge, raising funds for endless good causes, encouraging crafts of every description, caring for nature and the countryside and pioneering for the common good. I am moved to write about the ladies this week because on Wednesday evening they flung open their doors and invited everybody to an exhibition of how they have spent the years. It was all very impressive, and this month WIs everywhere will be doing something similar as part of a national promotion campaign. One of their leading lights said recently: 'This is the WI, and I am proud to be a member.' And I think there are plenty of chaps like me who would say: 'This is the WI, and I am proud to be a WI husband.'

William Condry

Snakes in the grass
⊰ May 1991 ⊱

To come across a new species of plant is always a pleasure, but to come across a meadow holding up to 300,000 of them is truly exciting, especially when it is a flower like the snake's-head fritillary. Its long, drooping, almost box-shaped bloom of light and dark purple chequering is one of the most spectacular in early spring and has attracted human attention for centuries.

The range of vernacular names, such as bloody warrior, widow wail, leopard's lily, toad's head, white pheasant's lily, weeping widow, and drooping bells of Sodom, is indicative of an almost animistic response to this curious flower. Bloody warrior, for instance, derived from a belief that it grew from drops of blood spilt by invading Danes. Like almost all plant species in southern Britain, *Fritillaria meleagris* has declined substantially in the last century. The Framsden colony, confined to a single riverside meadow of only 2.5 hectares, just east of Stowmarket, is now the largest in Suffolk. The ploughing, drainage and general 'improvement' of damp grasslands have destroyed 13 of an historical 17 fritillary sites in the county. Fortunately, three of the remaining four are now safely in the hands of the Suffolk Wildlife Trust. In conjunction with the owners of the farm encircling Fox Fritillary Meadow, the Trust organises an open day so that anyone can visit and enjoy the site.

Sadly, this year's generally dry conditions have encouraged the frit-illaries to flower earlier than usual, and to see them at their best will now involve an 11-month wait. However, the Trust holds other spectacular wild-flower meadows close to Framsden. Their most recent acquisition, opened only last week, is Winks Meadow near Harleston, which holds six species of orchid. The combination of interests that has worked to safeguard this site is indicative of the growing partnerships forged between the business, industrial and environmental communities. Owned by a group called Plantlife and run by the Suffolk Wildlife Trust, Winks Meadow was bought by the makers of Timotei shampoo.

Mark Cocker

The other Wimbledon

JULY 1991

Whilst tennis travailed through the rain Wimbledon Common cele-brated. Last summer's dryness is hard to remember as you watch a group of plump mistle thrushes pulling out worms from the damp ground. Here is no anxious search, but a confident stance and a steady stab. In open spaces the brambles show an abundance of enor-mous flowers.

Beyond the woodland, on the Iron Age fort, or 'Caesar's Camp', is an area covered in bloom. Yellows predominate: broom, creeping buttercups, drifts of black medick, and bird's-foot trefoil — some yellow, others remaining a strong orange picked up by the matt bottoms of the bumblebee *Bombus lapidarius* as they visit the flowers in the sunshine.

Small heath and holly blue butterflies flutter among the heady scents. Delicate grass vetchlings leave their clear crimson spot among the green. Geoffrey Grigson objected to this lovely plant having such 'a miserable book name' and called it Crimson Shoe. 'Now and again there are good (extra moist?) years in which Crimson Shoe will colour a whole patch of rough grass.' This is its year.

I even smiled blissfully at my arch enemy's close relation when I saw the neat flowers of the field bindweed adding their humble dash of white or pink. The wild lupins are out, cascades of leaves with delicate pinnacles of white or lilac flowers. All this wet abundance has filled my garden with slugs. Frogs lie about, defeated. A hemlock water dropwort growing by a pond is festooned with Sowerby's slugs with their orange keel, quite unaware of its 'Very Poisonous' description. The plant is ravaged, the slugs even sleeker. I encountered more odd behaviour from a Pembrokeshire field mouse.

Driving slowly along the farm road we spotted it on the track. We stopped. It continued nibbling. I got out, walked up to it, crouched down, put out my hand, stroked its whiskers. It turned to sniff me, started to walk on to the hand, changed its mind, nibbled a bit more, moved over to the bank and vanished.

Audrey Insch

Hedges and sedges
❧ NOVEMBER 1992 ❧

A man mending a roof at Ampleforth complained to southern visitors below that North Yorkshire was 'nowt but bloody views'. My grandmother made the opposite kind of complaint from the passenger seat of an elderly Austin 7 on a rare expedition into the Kentish lanes: 'You'd think the hedgers and ditchers had all dropped dead.' She couldn't see the view. Somerset has the balance right, especially just now. Though I have several times passed a man bent in a ditch, grubbing it out with a primitive implement, there's little call for hedgers and ditchers these days where the two-handed engine deployed by the local authority gouges the ditches and trims the hedges to regulation size and shape. When, too, solid masses of foliage have thinned, or disappeared, to expose the magnificent framework of the trees, there is a remarkable opening-up of views on every side. And the mixture varies between hills, little hollows, and large flat spaces like 'the Levels', where Monmouth's peasants were cut down at the battle of Sedgemoor, and, in the south, running into Dorset, Blackmoor Vale. Hardy says that, as you approach the Vale's southern edge, it spreads out like a map, and the same is true as you drop down from Wincanton, or the high vantage-point at Cucklington, by stages, through Templecombe. Just a few miles away is the inn where Tess's father over-indulged, and through those lanes Tess travelled sleepily at two or three in the morning to catch the market at Casterbridge, when the silent mail-cart, speeding through the dark, speared her old horse and started her chain of disaster. Our friendly red mail van buzzes briskly from village to village through the lanes, but at a later, safer hour, and, thanks to the hedge-trimming machine, with a better field of vision on the corners. And now we can see through the spaces the clean, slender lines of Evercreech's famous perpendicular tower, sharpened by the low sunshine, and the shapes of stone barns, farms, and houses that fit the landscape with a rightness to make a planning officer weep.

John Vallins

The peanut mystery
◆ JUNE 1993 ◆

A few days at home gave me the opportunity of solving a wildlife mystery associated with the bird table that we now stock with appropriate food all the year round. Under the large bird table are four bags of peanuts and three of them gradually empty over about three days under the seemingly constant attention by siskins, chaffinches, greenfinches and three species of tits. The fourth bag takes just over a day to empty and after watching the table I realised it was a male great spotted woodpecker and the mystery was why it only goes for that one bag of peanuts. I noticed that the bottom of the bags of peanuts were all at a different height from the large stone under them. Only one bag was in the right position so that the woodpecker could use its still tail feathers on the stone to help support it as it hung from the bag of nuts. Another interesting observation was that when the woodpecker had finished feeding it would drop to the stone below and gather up a beak full of small pieces of peanuts it had scattered and then it was off – no doubt feeding the pieces to the female in the nest hole that we suspect is in an oak at the far end of the paddock. As if this was not delightful enough there has been an equally attractive coloured bird in the form of a drake mandarin duck that loafs around the edge of the larger of our three garden ponds. His close attention to the pond is because the female mandarin duck is incubating eggs in a nest box only a few yards from the pond. In contrast early one morning I watched a male redstart take a caterpillar into a nest box where the female is incubating eggs. All the other small nest boxes in the garden are empty as in the spring all the resident tits – and siskins – were taken by two sparrowhawks. The peanuts and lower part of the bird table are now enmeshed with two-inch-hole wire and this has made the sparrowhawks go elsewhere. I know my attitude is not logical!

Ray Collier

The deepest-ever diary
ꙮ June 1994 ꙮ

We entered the rusty cage of Pit B at Monkwearmouth colliery on a rescue mission, in search of an underground colony of shrimps that has persisted since the shaft was sunk in 1826. After a 12-minute descent we jerked to a halt 1,080 feet underground, stepping out into caverns lined with crystals that glistened in our lamp beams. We found the colony, in a small black lagoon at a tunnel entrance littered with rusty picks and blocked by a collapsed roof. The half-inch-long shrimps dashed across the surface, flashing through pools of light from our helmets and disappearing into the black ooze. These tiny crustaceans, familiar to generations of Wearmouth miners, live in a seasonless world of perpetual darkness and constant temperature, probably feeding on bacteria that grow on sulphur in the coal. Kenny Drysdale, the shaftsman who led us to them, told us that miners once supplemented the shrimps' diet with bread crusts. Within a few minutes we had scooped up as many animals as we could catch. The only other sign of life was a spider's web. Its builder, long-since gone, must have been drawn down by the shaft ventilation system. In the tunnels we passed massive, rusty iron grates where fires had once burned, to draw in cold ventilating air from above in the wake of their rising column of heat. Then, this pit must have resembled a scene from the underworld. The names of generations of miners were chalked or scratched on walls and beams in silent tunnels strewn with rusty pulleys and rails, thick with dust, shored up with props and baulks and boards and sealed with crumbling doors that hung from creaking hinges. Back on the surface, the rescued shrimps now live in my laboratory, thriving in an aquarium. In a few weeks the unlucky ones will be sealed underground for ever, when the life of the colliery finally expires. Yesterday, I dropped a crust of bread into the tank. The shrimps swarmed around, tore crumbs off and retreated to their corners, just as Kenny said they would.

Phil Gates

D-Day naturalist
❧ JUNE 1994 ❧

In 1932 I gave my brother, two years my senior, *The Ornithologists'
Field Book*. The preliminary list of British birds was duly ticked off as his
records increased, but the main part of the book, lined blank pages,
was untouched for the following 12 years. Ian, a telegraphist, had
joined the London Fire Service at the outbreak of war, but getting
bored during the period before the blitz, managed to resign and join
the RAF. From then on his lips were sealed, we assumed that he was
connected with a hush-hush service involving usually airforce uni-
forms but sometimes khaki with an anchor emblem on the shoulder –
hints of what we came to know as Combined Ops. I took possession of
his bird diary after his death a few years ago, and found that he had
written it up almost daily since his arrival in Normandy on June 7. The
entries were terse, such as 'Good dry landing – shot at by E-boat on
way, and a sniper on landing. Bout of digging our lovely dugout. Noisy
night.' But in the early days there was no mention of birds and it was
only in later conversations I learned that he had flushed a peregrine on
the final ascent of the cliff, and though tempted to look for the nest,
continued his hurried upward journey. No hints as to the activities of
his group, but when he was demobbed all came out – his was a very
secret unit with a waggon containing the newly invented radar appa-
ratus. He loved telling of how they were instructed to let no one in,
not even the C in C, without written authorisation. Later Ian seemed
to pay greater attention to birds, and was very impressed by a noisy
night of Manx shearwater calls, with which he had become familiar on
a joint visit to the Pembroke island of Skokholm. There were refer-
ences to passages of migrants like yellow wagtails, wheatears, and
redstarts. Ian returned home unscathed except for a broken wrist
from a champagne-induced tumble from a lorry. His next bird note of
interest was of black redstarts nesting high up on Paddington Station.

W.D. Campbell

A Hundred Up

On a bright May day in 1996, the London editor of the Country
Diary section of the *Guardian*, Jeannette Page, dug a spade
deep into a layer of Oxfordshire soil and so officially opened the
W.D. Campbell Copse. The small wood which now thrives on the
Mill Field at Charlbury in Oxfordshire – the 'little town' which Bill
Campbell described weekly for nearly 25 of his 30 diary years – is the
most recent of a series of memorials to writers who have contributed
to the column. You can walk in them, watch birds from them, drink
beer from them or skinny-dip in them with no one watching if you
don't mind the cold of a Lake District tarn at over 1500 feet above
sea level.

The practice began on Thomas Coward's death. The first of all the
diary writers was the subject of a national memorial appeal within
months. Donations came in from all over the world, including China,
the United States, India and Australia, and more than £900 was

raised, the equivalent of almost £50,000 today. The money was used to buy Cotterill Clough near the present site of Manchester Airport and a large reedbed – favoured resort of the diary's famous great crested grebes – on Budworth Mere. You can still inspect the quiet landscape and its wildlife from the T.A. Coward Memorial Bird Hide. Coward's heir on the Cheshire beat, Arnold Boyd, is likewise remembered by the A.W. Boyd Memorial Observatory in the Rostherne national nature reserve. Finished in 1962, three years after his death, it had to be extended a decade later because it was so popular with birders. To complete a Cheshire *Guardian* triumvirate, Boyd's own successor L.P. Samuels organised a monthly flushing out of wildfowl round the mere, so that colleagues in the Boyd Observatory could keep a species and population count.

Harry Griffin wasn't at all pleased when the time came for a memorial to his work, somewhat prematurely because he was still very much alive. His great interest in tarns – the 'eyes of the mountain', he called them, borrowing the phrase from the painter William Heaton Cooper – prompted some fans to suggest in 2003 that an anonymous stretch of water at the head of Greenburn in the fells behind Grasmere should be named Griffin Tarn. 'I am dead against this,' he wrote in a Country Diary. 'And not just because the pool is pretty undistinguished and dreary. I thank my correspondents for their zeal, but this should remain a joke.' There almost certainly will be a Griffin Tarn before the century is much older. But meanwhile a different and very welcome liquid tribute is available in honour of Ted Ellis. As one of the most knowledgeable and enthusiastic naturalists to be based in East Anglia, he has been honoured by a bottled beer, the Ted Ellis special from Wolf's brewery, which has his twinkly face peering out from the label at all who buy it. Ted is also commemorated by a house at Wymondham comprehensive school and the sticks whirled by the Morris dancers Kemp's Men of Norwich, which are renewed with funds from his estate. Appropriately, one of the current diarists, Phil Gates, who is senior lecturer in botany at Durham University, is immortalised by an A-level biology exam question based on his fascinating account of shrimps in Monkwearmouth coal mine, physically the deepest diary ever written. Students still tell him how they remember it, and the underlying point about isolated animal populations, from exam practice at school.

The past is never as important as the future in journalism, however, and the diary's run-in to its centenary in 2004 saw a further increase in its band of writers. Stalwarts such as Harry Griffin, heading for his half-centenary as a diarist in 2001, were joined by more colleagues than ever before, some of them for relatively short runs. When the milestone was reached, there were ten of them sharing diary duties and a stable editing system under Celia Locks, after an interregnum when a sometimes haphazard rota of sub-editors handled the column. The diarists' subject had a permanent place among the top half-dozen issues on the national agenda and there was newly healthy competition, with the likes of Germaine Greer writing the *Times*'s much younger column, Nature Notes. The whole country appeared to pitch in on controversies from GM crops to the farming of animals for medical experiments. The return of foot-and-mouth in 2001 and the great debates over fox-hunting and the right to roam attracted all but universal interest. Lush Places had never been the backwater of Evelyn Waugh's imagination, but now it had demonstrably serious responsibilities.

Perhaps the most important of these had echoes of Thomas Coward's nervous refusal to share his conservation-minded views with Farmer Nicholson on the diary's launch 100 years earlier. By the late 1990s, farming had ceased to be the main countryside employer in Britain, albeit that it was still highly productive. Even in the rural county of North Yorkshire, the number of people employed in the voluntary and charitable sector overtook the total working in agriculture. Tourism was much larger. As the Countryside Alliance complained during its campaign against the fox-hunting ban, Merrie

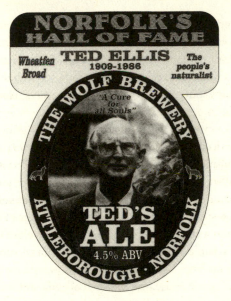

Every journalist's dream — Ted Ellis has been immortalised by a brand of beer

England was at risk of being redefined by those who only visited, and did not live there. An interesting if perhaps insoluble example of the different views which resulted came when Colin Luckhurst seemed to credit a tractor-driving friend with a mystical ability to assess soil fertility. A reader wrote in crisply: 'The Bible, common sense and O level biology indicate the potential riches of a fallow field.'

In these circumstances, it was a blessing for the diary to have writers such as Pete Bowler, who was strongly conservationist but addressed the rural issues of his native North Derbyshire and South Yorkshire with a self-taught expertise of the kind which *Guardian* editors going back to C.P. Scott had always treasured. Bowler left school at 16 to make bicycle frames and then sell soap, both of which he did badly because he was always playing truant to inspect threatened landscapes and wildlife. His classrooms were the old pitheaps of the area, gradually reverting to nature, where he learned to find all manner of plants, animals – and their traces. Forty years later, as one of the region's most respected environmental consultants, he liked to say: 'Show me a pile of crap, and I'll show you what did it.' It is impossible not to be scatological when discussing Pete, who asked to be described on his death certificate as 'shit-stirrer'.

That was not because of his expertise in animal faeces but a reference to his ruthless but always fair and knowledgeable campaigning, variously as a Liberal councillor, member of Yorkshire Wildlife Trust and, most famously, scourge of the newly privatised water companies during the Great Yorkshire Drought of 1994–5. He bridged the gap between country people and town visitors by understanding both but also cautioning them on inaccuracies. History often came to his help. He was expert at showing how an apparently 'wild' patch of South Yorkshire was actually the artificial product of ancient draining, coppicing or other human intervention. Contrariwise, he introduced many outsiders to the glorious countryside of an area often wrongly perceived as overwhelmingly industrial.

Cancer got Pete at the age of only 52 in September 2005 but his green burial in a beautiful, peaceful valley – although in a crook of the M1 motorway and only a few miles away from Sheffield and Rotherham – was a perfect Country Diary occasion. Wildflowers were blooming, the sun shone and every 'green' group in the region you could think of joined a procession of speakers to make impromptu tributes, after the manner of a Quaker meeting. Pete had been iffy about the imminent prospect of a new 'shrunken' *Guardian* but he would have been delighted to see the column back on the leader page, after its long exile. It was also a measure of his influence, and that of the diary more widely, that among messages enquiring about working as his successor was one from a government minister newly returned to the backbenches.

Ruins of the mine

❧ FEBRUARY 1995 ❧

Winter brings a welcome return of Cornwall's Kneehigh Theatre to Calstock and, on an unseasonally mild Saturday night, we walk there through the woods from Calstock. The near-full moon partially obscured by thin, slow-moving clouds sheds a wan light and, from beneath the high garden wall bounding Cotehele House, the orange street lights of riverside Calstock are clearly visible, rising in tiers above the Tamar. Below the path, inside a chestnut paling, the carp-pool reflects a rectangle of pale sky and the dovecote's smooth dome rises from a darker tangle of shrubs. The path curves steeply down a wooded river-cliff where leaning, ivyed trunks of gnarled oaks are silhouetted against sky and high-tide water below. Apart from the caw of a stray rook it is quiet and very still but, as we descend carefully over slippery, glistening slate and knotted tree roots, quietness is replaced by the turbulence of Danescombe stream rushing to join the calmer tidal river. Across the stream a level track continues past old miners' cottages and quays where granite, copper and other ores were once loaded on to sailing barges. The square bulk of a lime-kiln looms close by, water dripping from its cavernous roof and trickling out of rock-faces. Now our footsteps echo under the arch of the derelict incline railway, its walls shining with patches of crystallised oozing lime. Then high above river and houses the two-coached 7 p.m. train, from Gunnislake to Plymouth, glides across the graceful viaduct towards the darker Devon side. Here, on the Cornish bank, opposite reed beds and woods, in the centre of Calstock are car park, social club emanating rock 'n' roll music with flashing lights, and village hall where people eagerly await *The Ash Maid*, Kneehigh's rendition of the magical tale of Cinderella. For the next two hours we will be captivated and enthralled by these master storytellers who will enchant their audience with a sparkling performance in the best tradition of travelling players.

Virginia Spiers

Monitoring moths
❧ MARCH 1996 ❧

A review of moth records in Cheshire during 1995, by Ian Rutherford, the county recorder, appears in the spring issue of the Lancashire and Cheshire Entomological Society newsletter. Reports during the first five months of the year were far from encouraging, with the prospect of 1995 being another poor year for the county. Spring appearances and counts were low, and in some quarters, usually plentiful species were not seen at all – Pale Brindled Beauty and Twin-spot Quaker being two examples notable by their absence from the author's own trap. Once into and through June the weather improved, as did the records, with reports of large catches and a wide range of species which added over 100 new sightings to the 10-km-square recording base. However, the improvement did not last into the autumn when catches were again widely noted below the normal average. Amongst the successes during the summer was the addition of three species to the county list – a Silver Hook was taken on mossland in the north of the county, and the same trap produced Lempke's Gold Spot, a moth whose previous absence had long puzzled the reviewer. The third, found in the extreme west, was an Orache Moth, a species extinct as a resident in the UK for more than a century, and today recorded on extremely rare occasions as an immigrant. The Orache was seen in July and another rare immigrant, a Striped Hawk, was reported in early October, but apart from these two, as the review states, '. . . we saw very little else in the moth line to compare with the invasion by Camberwell Beauty Butterflies and Yellow-winged Darter Dragonflies . . .' As to the most important record of 1995, this was the discovery of a nest of larvae of the Small Eggar, a nationally scarce moth whose serious decline is attributed to pollution and the wholesale destruction of our hedgerows.

John Thompson

From ooze to river

❧ JULY 1997 ☙

From afar, the Wrekin and its surrounding wooded hills have all but vanished under a shifting, smoky cape of cloud. Inside, the woods are dank and gloriously sodden. The air is spicy with the sharp green scent of bracken, the sticky sweetness of honeysuckle drapes and hidden stinkhorn. Within this humid wood-mist, the fungi are stirring early from damp loam and rotten logs. Out in the open, in the regenerating quarry valley in Maddocks Hill, is a spectacular display of common spotted orchids. An ooze from the quarry floor determines a new path, joining run-off from woods and lanes to drain into a little wet woodland. Beneath a canopy of alders these trickles merge into a narrow stream, which leads to one of those uniquely secretive places: an old yew tree twists out of the stream bed surrounded by a muddy pool with tussock sedge. From this swamp, the stream passes under the road to plunge into the narrow gorge of the Forest Glen. Water from the north end of the Wrekin flows north through the Forest Glen, into the old reservoir, out through Cluddley and along the west side of Wellington, as the Beanhill Brook, before entering the River Tern in the Weald Moors and eventually the Severn at Atcham. Here in the woods of Hazel Hurst, at the foot of the Wrekin, the recent rains begin that journey with a strange and rare song. This is the wild, indecipherable song of nameless streams, where few paths cross but none follow. A song which bubbles and pours over stones, roots and mossy logs; deep and throaty in its narrow trough; thick and leafy under a green shade. A rare song because summer rains have in recent years been ephemeral, but this year's are persistent, strident, scouring the stream beds in a cleansing tide. This is the cold, clear life-blood the ancients may have drunk here from a skull.

Paul Evans

Prince of whales
᠀ JULY 1998 ᠀

The minke whale is a difficult beast to try to convey. By the standards of the rest of its awesome family, the six species of rorqual whale, it is not so remarkable. The adults average 8–9 metres in length and weigh around 5–7 tonnes. Compare this with the 26 metres and 100 tonnes of its relative, the blue whale, and a minke seems a mere baby. But when we saw them recently at the magical Rua Reigh lighthouse in Wester Ross, they were big enough to leave us gasping with excitement. They are the largest mammal you are likely to see from British soil, and the stretch of Atlantic known as the Minch, between the Hebridean island of Lewis and the Scottish mainland, is an excellent place to observe them. When we visited, a combination of uninterrupted sunshine and an ocean panorama which was as calm as a South Sea lagoon were nearly perfect conditions for watching cetaceans.

Most of the time the minkes simply rose to breathe, appearing as a long convex line of black at the surface. Occasionally, we caught a spout of misty spray and just once – for several glorious seconds – a minke rose from the waters, its whole upper body thrusting sky-wards in one almighty surge. How extraordinary to think that further north the Norwegians are still hunting minkes for their blubber. One Norwegian foreign minister referred to the minkes as 'rats of the sea' and accused them 'of taking fish from fishermen'. In defiance of the International Whaling Commission, the Norwegians set their 1998 quota at 671 minkes. This is based on their 1995 estimate of the North Atlantic population at 118,000 – a census widely condemned as grossly exaggerating true numbers. To give you an idea of the imprecision of whale estimates, in one area of the Barents Sea, sightings of just 29 whales were the basis for a calculation in that area of a population of 16,101 minkes.

Mark Cocker

A woewater omen
❧ MARCH 1999 ❧

There was talk in the pub in the Chilterns that our local woewater had reappeared. The glinting ribbon of water had been glimpsed snaking down between the woods from the chalk hills to the south, and we all tried to remember when it last flowed. These winterbournes are a feature of chalk country, and they tend to spring up in late winter after periods of heavy rains. The aquifers become full, and the water bursts out, typically at the junction between two different rock strata. Gilbert White, of Selborne, wrote about the Hampshire landsprings, which he called by the local vernacular name lavants, and described how they presaged poor harvests. 'The country people say when the lavants rise corn will always be dear meaning that when the earth is so glutted with water as to send forth springs on the downs and uplands, that the corn-vales must be drowned.' Perhaps this is why they were sometimes seen as omens of bad luck in a more general sense, and ours acquired the reputation of being a woewater, predictive of wars and disasters. But it last flowed in 1988, and before that in April 1975, just before the fighting stopped in Vietnam. This year's proved to be a modest flow, some of it underground. But in 1988 the bourne gushed and bubbled like a mountain torrent, flooded whole fields, and suddenly made sense of the geography of the prehistoric dry valley in which it flows. And to this ephemeral wet landscape came snipe and heron, just as if it were a proper marsh.

Richard Mabey

A secret sex life
❧ MARCH 1999 ❧

The wood anemones in Hollingside Wood at Durham are poised to spread their flower petals at the first hint of warm sunlight. The bluebell leaves have speared through the decaying leaf litter and their flower buds are just visible. But for one group of plants here – the ferns – the annual race to reproduce is over already. Ferns are plants with a secret sex life, accomplished without the help of flowers, that passes unnoticed unless you know where and when to look. Late last summer tens of thousands of tiny spore cases on the underside of fern fronds burst and catapulted out dust-like spores that blew across the woodland floor. By late autumn they had germinated into a microscopic thread of green cells, broadening as the weeks passed into heart-shaped membrane – a prothallus – green, rootless and fragile, just one cell thick and not much bigger than a baby's finger-nail. On the top, egg cells formed in tiny, long-necked flasks called archegonia. Underneath the male cells – antherozoids – multiplied, packed inside minute barrel-shaped containers.

On a mild, wet day in late autumn or early winter (all this can only happen in wet surroundings – even a brief drought is fatal) the containers burst, unleashing swarms of swimming male antherozoids that gyrated in the surface film of water, racing towards the egg cells along an attractive gradient of organic acids oozing from the necks of the archegonia. It all happened in the depths of winter, on a scale so small that only a powerful microscope could have made it visible, but I found the telltale evidence on the soggy, rotten trunk of a fallen elm. There were the clusters of new fern plants – fronds just a few centimetres tall – sprouting from withering prothalli where the antherozoids had made their short, frantic journey.

Phil Gates

Protecting a patch
❧ MAY 1999 ❧

Pulfin, a corruption of Pool Fen, must be the best marshland of its type in Yorkshire. Thirty-eight acres of reed and reed canary grass sit on top of sedge peat, within a meander of the River Hull. With the river on three sides, its fourth side is protected by an esker, a glacial moraine. Nearby, the village of Eske retains the geographic link.

We were there to examine ways of further protecting and enhancing this very important wildlife site. In the droughts of 1989–92 and 95–96, the peat springs which well up from underground aquifers failed and the peat began to dry out. Areas which became dry have been invaded by great hairy willowherb. The patches of meadow rue, meadowsweet, yellow loosestrife, marsh woundwort and marsh marigold have been reduced.

Despite there being an adjacent borrow-pit, which is used for flood control, we have been unable to gain access to the water to keep Pulfin wetted at times of drought. Drainage of the surrounding land, and over abstraction from the underground chalk aquifer mean that the springs will fail again in dry years. Attempts to purchase and lease additional parcels of land which will give us the ability to manage water levels better, have met with unrealistic conditions and prices.

It was still great to be out on the reed swamp on this bright, sunny day. A pair of turtle doves, summer visitors and a species under threat, flew into a nearby willow, and a cuckoo flew across our line of vision, pursued by a thrush. Our movement through the reeds flushed out a water rail, a secretive enough bird at the best of times. This one had been making its distinctive groaning calls in the vegetation for a while, then flew up a foot or two above the reeds for a short distance, before dropping back into cover and scuttling away.

Having enjoyed a few hours of sun and tranquillity on this tiny corner of historical landscape, we went off to plan its protection. Instead of more hours in the sunshine, we will be spending days in meetings, negotiating, proposing, persuading.

Pete Bowler

Freewheeling

❧ AUGUST 1999 ❧

Boats and bicycles, Holland revels in them all. Cyclists have their own tracks, their own traffic lights and their own position on the roads. Dutch bicycles are what we might call old-fashioned. Forget the low-slung racing idea, unless you are a low-slung racer. Think instead of sitting up above the world, your back straight, your hands resting on high handlebars. If you want to stop when you are on one of these you have to leave the saddle and slip a foot on to the ground. Otherwise you move majestically forward, able to view the goings-on around you as if from a silent mobile hide. Birds don't bother looking. Blue and purple herons stand in the meadows by the river Vecht, peer into ditches or perch unforgettably on thick water-lily roots in the middle of lakes, apparently standing on water. You see no hills, only trees in the distance. So many Dutch paintings spring to mind. And sky: you see the clouds forming and moving, dissolving, falling on you, all from your throne. Never once did I see a cycle helmet.

Sailing may be the best transport here. A light wind and away you go. On the Loosdrechste Plassen there is an area of water where engines are not allowed. There you move through water lilies and ducks, crested grebes and dragonflies, their wings clashing in hot pursuit. If you put out an anchor the ducks snuffle the water around you, their beady eyes watching every biscuit you happen to pick up. Meanwhile, small green damselflies cluster around, curious about the strange creatures they're meeting. Close by we spoke to a man on a houseboat who keeps chickens, pheasants and geese for fun. At the eclipse, so he told us, all his birds did what was expected of them and turned in for bed. One night we walked on a straight road beside the Grachje, a small canal linking the river and the huge Amsterdam-Rhein Kanaal and heard the glorious sound of lapwings calling from the meadows.

Audrey Insch

208

Soap from seeds

Along the canals and riverbanks on the north-western fringes of Rotherham, soapwort is enjoying its last few days of flowering. A member of the pink family, it isn't widespread in the British Isles, but owes its presence here in South Yorkshire to commercial growing. Not for the horticultural trade, but for the woollen industry of 200 years ago. When bruised and boiled in water, the fleshy green parts of the plant produce a liquid soft soap, hence its common name. Apparently, it was brought to Britain during the Middle Ages from the continent, presumably as the woollen industry grew and prospered. Why is this flower on the edge, even in the centre, of a town noted more for its iron and coal industry than for agriculture? The answer is that 250 years ago, it was grown commercially on the slopes of the Don Valley. In Sheffield city archives, there is a mid-18th-century map showing the area around Droppingwell. On either side of Green Lane, an ancient trackway leading towards the Pennines, were fields marked 'Soapfield'. Others nearby were marked pasture or coppice. Whether the crop for these soapfields was used locally is a matter of conjecture, but it is a relatively short wagon journey from Droppingwell, over through Penistone to Holmfirth and sheep country.

It is suggested that soapwort is a native plant of Devon and Cornwall, and well it may be. Here in South Yorkshire the seed-pods often fail to ripen, but it spreads vegetatively via creeping rhizomes. That they are typically found close to watercourses suggests that the network of colonisation is via broken roots washed up in suitable places having been carried downstream on floodwaters. Flowering from late June through to the very end of October, soapwort blooms in vast swathes of pink and white flowers. Even its fleshy, light green leaves stand out as you walk along the pathways.

Just imagine what a whole field would have looked like, before being harvested and carted up the valley to wash the wool that produced the wealth which built Huddersfield, Halifax, Leeds and Bradford.

Pete Bowler

Secrecy for sale
❧ FEBRUARY 2001 ☙

The recent news that the shooting rights are for sale on one of the last forbidden bastions in the southern Pennines is most interesting. Wanderers on the broad heather moors of Snailsden have always had to run the gauntlet. Its privacy has been strictly enforced; Snailsden is a byword for exclusion. The 4,000-acre moor also has the distinction of being one of the first places to practise grouse driving, in about 1842. In keeping with national trends, the game records for Snailsden over the last quarter-century show a generally declining annual crop of grouse shot – 528 brace in 1975, 94 brace in 2000, though, of course, there are large variations from year to year. There are no public rights of way over the moor and this has long been a bone of contention, when ramblers have struck out across the line of grouse butts heading, maybe, for the far-off sentinel of the Holme Moss television mast and so upset sitting grouse. There have been periodic angry confrontations with the keeper and his beaters when trespassers have come striding across the head of Ramsden Clough, heading for the upper reaches of Winscar Reservoir. Here, too, is the source of the River Don, on the lonely, moortop crest of Withens Edge. It starts as a trickle burbling east to flow into an arm of Winscar Reservoir almost within sight of the gamekeeper's cottage at Wetshaw Edge.

There is a hopeful note in the sale particulars, however. It states that Yorkshire Water, as freeholders of Snailsden Moor, wish to designate a linear footpath here, though the proposed route has yet to be finalised. The northern edge of the moor falls away to small head-water valleys draining to the Holme Valley, and they are enhanced by blocks of coniferous plantations around little reservoirs originally built to provide mill water. I remember a fine spring evening when we crossed in an almost straight line from Holme Moss to the rocky declivities of Ramsden Clough. Then we cut across to the public road close to the site of the long-vanished Cook's Study, former shooting lodge and observatory of the Stanhopes. The grouse were calling in the soft, slanting sunlight; a cuckoo sang far away towards Holme. We didn't, though, see any sign of the keeper or hear shouts to get off these precious sporting wastes.

Roger Redfern

Banned from the fells
MARCH 2001

Denied access to the fells recently – in superb winter conditions, with sunlit snows and extensive distant views – we were reduced, the other day, to a few miles' saunter along Morecambe Promenade. But at least there were views of the snowbound Lakeland fells across the water, the shrimpers out on the edge of the sands, huge, wheeling flocks of birds quartering the bay, and plenty of fresh air. On the way, we had passed the shore at Hest Bank and seen dozens of walkers far out on the sands – an inspiration for later walks. We could tackle the fascinating coastline, exploring for miles, and keep well away from fell and farmland. Several times we encountered other walkers, in boots and balaclavas, and exchanged smiles and wry glances. No need for words. We were all on the same job – seeking a bit of exercise away from the hills. How well I remember the last foot-and-mouth epidemic in 1967, when we were denied the fells for the whole of November and December, and only allowed back again halfway through January — a very long deprivation that tested us sorely. Will the present restrictions last as long? — or longer? The current outbreak is much more widespread than the one 34 years ago, which was mostly confined to Cheshire and Shropshire. Of course, I remember the exasperation of 1967, but people complied with the regulations and certainly the fells were quite deserted for 10 weeks. But, mostly, I recall that November 1967 was, infuriatingly, a superb month, with day after day of unbroken, late autumn sunshine, little wind and superb views.

Harry Griffin

Murder most royal
JULY 2002

During the hotter days of summer, I find things go a bit haywire, skew-whiff, odd to say the least. One such day began in the greenhouse. Watering the plants usually brings out the greenhouse gaffer, a spider the size of a baby's fist, from her lair. When drops of water hit the web, stretched around the tubular entrance to her secret world, she pounces in a split second to see if it is something she should kill. When she didn't appear I checked her web and found an enormous hornet, *Vespa crabo*. Appropriately named after an Italian motor scooter, this fantastic creature was obviously a queen. She lay in state, trapped in gossamer, bent double with an abdomen like plates of polished leather, and dark bladed wings folded back. Had two fearsome queens, the spider and the hornet, killed each other in what must have been a terrifying regicidal struggle? Hornets are very uncommon here, in fact I've never seen one in this immediate area before. As the climate warms, we can expect more such insects further north than their usual range. Perhaps the future of an advance colony of hornets here has been arrested by this murder.

There was something deadly in the stifling silence of the greenhouse

*Pete Bowler at one of his favourite haunts, the threatened
peat bogs of Thorne Waste in South Yorkshire*

which reached eerily into the outside world. From trees above, a
wood pigeon offered its soft bluesy five-note call, again and again and
again. After the battle of the queens I hoped for something more
bardic, the complex and ominous song of the wren perhaps. But no,
only this monotonous apparently dull pigeon voice had anything to
say in the hot summer air.

Paul Evans

Newts are not daft
❧ MARCH 2003 ☙

The emergence of newts from their winter hibernation tends to go
unremarked. They are less visible, less noisy and go about their egg-
laying less immediately, and in a more individual manner, than frogs. Yet

they are on the move. At Ellerton, near the Derwent river, civil engineers have been replacing the old sewer overflow for Yorkshire Water. To prevent newts from entering the excavation, an exclusion fence was erected, with smooth plastic sheeting buried into the ground. A series of pitfall traps pick up any newts emerging from the working area.

Through most of February, the freezing weather ensured that no newt was daft enough to emerge from hibernation. The weekend's rain and warmer temperatures changed all that; on the last day, the pitfall traps revealed that five smooth newts — four male and one female — had fallen in on their nightly journey.

Lifting the plastic sheeting out of its buried, shallow trench, we found eight more — six males and two females. An interesting gender ratio; perhaps the males want to get to the pond first to pick the best courting spots. Already, the largest males are developing the crest along their backs — their breeding plumage. If you have never seen a great crested newt, it is easy to assume that these are they; once seen, the bigger, wartier, uglier great-crested species makes future identification easy.

Leaving Ellerton, my attention was caught by a dead pheasant on the roadside. A sandy-coloured weasel was vigorously tugging at its wing, dragging the carcass to the verge. I saw the weasel break off the wing, scamper over the verge, across the ditch and into the hedge bottom, where it cached its prize. Returning, using fresh mole hills as cover, it dragged the remaining body a bit further, then broke off another joint, caching that a little further along the hedge. Thus lightened, the corpse was pulled off the road, bobbing behind the weasel into the ditch.

Pete Bowler

Jumble Hole
❧ NOVEMBER 2003 ☙

In the upper reaches of the Calder Valley lies Jumble Hole Clough, a steep wooded valley embracing a fast-flowing stream which tumbles off the high moorland. Near the head of the clough stands a mute reminder of the early days of the Industrial Revolution, in the shape of ruins of a small water-powered mill which is slowly being engulfed by the surrounding foliage. The ruins evoke a time before the growth of the larger mills, which sprang up along the banks of the River Calder with the advent of mechanisation as transport links were developed. Shoehorned into the valley bottom now are road, railway, river and canal. Jumble Hole is one of several such cloughs in the area and they provide seclusion, as well as a haven, for wildlife.

A pleasing walk is to access the clough via the canal towpath from Hebden Bridge from where there is a good chance of spotting the unmistakable azure flash that is the kingfisher. The recent RSPB report on the encouraging increase in the number of this most handsome of birds is borne out by recent sightings both on the canal and the adjacent River Calder. Passing through the hilltop village of Blackshaw Head, one soon reaches the wild, wide open spaces of Heptonstall Moor, from where the panorama includes the distant obelisk of Stoodley Pike, perched high above the valley overlooking Todmorden. The pike is situated on the Pennine Way, visible for miles, and there are spectacular views from its stone balcony.

The return route to Hebden Bridge is through Hardcastle Crags, another striking wooded valley at the heart of which lies Gibson Mill. A recent TV adaptation of a Dickens novel featured scenes shot at the mill, which stands on the banks of Hebden Water. Further downstream is a squirrel-proof bird feeder fixed to a telegraph pole, where a nuthatch or greater spotted woodpecker will attach itself and crane its neck into the feeder, seemingly oblivious to the frantic feeding of the smaller birds.

Peter Stowe

On the Gwent levels

The Gwent Levels Wetland Reserve can be a cold place in a south-east wind on a mid-November afternoon. We pull our coats more tightly around us as a gust bends the dry reeds that edge the long lagoon. The reserve stretches about three miles along the Severn Estuary, from Uskmouth to Goldcliff. Built to compensate for the loss of rich feeding areas for waders and wild fowl when the Barrage was completed across Cardiff Bay, it has become a place of reedbeds, lagoons, wet grasslands and saltmarsh – all this, under a wide estuarial sky. Today the November light is weak, and only isolated shafts of sunlight pierce the cloud. There is a flat greyness to the whole estuary, which on sunny days can be transformed into a band of gleaming silver. A single pool of sunlight lights up a patch of sea far across the channel, and on the horizon a cargo ship, its outline softened by distance, waits for the tide, which will soon spill across the mudflats and salt marsh.

Along the water's edge groups of wigeon, teal, shelduck, mallard and waders feed; the wings of a flock of dunlin flash white against the grey mud as they turn to settle. A single curlew trails its liquid song across the marsh. We continue along the sea wall until the need for hot coffee becomes imperative, and then we sit for a while. The sun, lower now, picks out the intricate tracery of runnels that drain through the grass to the tide edge. When we finally return, we decide to take a path between two of the longest lagoons. High above our heads the starlings have begun to gather along the wires and arms of two huge pylons. They come, flock on flock, from all directions, low and urgent, until the arms are festooned in birds, and the cables seem strung with dark beads. Around them the main flock, now thousands-strong, is a black, ever evolving, ever changing shape. Controlled, ordered, as some strange avian dynamic arranges and rearranges the three-dimensional magic of the huge flock. As we watch, the light fades, and the birds stream away over a belt of low trees to their roost. By the time that we reach the car, the last of the light has gone.

Philip Price

Bones of the past
❧ DECEMBER 2003 ☙

When the wind sweeps over the common, the high bank along the River Ivel is an unforgiving place. Even the willow trees offer no shelter, instead raking the walker with thin twigs like spiteful witches' brooms. Thankfully, today is frosty calm. Festooned on the branches dangling over the river, ancient flood-borne vegetation hangs limply, like tired Christmas tinsel. The walk along the Ivel is a gentle stroll, so much so that earlier this year I followed its course, in just a day, from the chalk stream in the Chiltern foothills outside Baldock, to the point on the Cambridgeshire border just short of St Neots where it is swallowed up in the mighty Ouse.

The ease of the walk is no happy accident; this raised, flattened bank was once a busy canal towpath. Reaching the concrete weir, the river divides, one fork snaking in front of the old manor house before plunging down another weir into the millpool. The path, however, hugs the bank along the new cut, a channel dug for the canal opening in 1758.

What evidence remains of the thriving waterway that once carried goods out, via the Ouse, to the port of Wisbech? Here, at the weir, our amateur detective curiosity has given us a remarkable find. Lying forgotten at the base of a gnarled hawthorn bush, some 20 yards back from the water, is an enormous beam, about 1ft thick and 8ft in length.

This timber is clearly part of a lock gate, ripped out and dumped on the common when the canal closed in 1876. The agents of oblivion are returning the wood inexorably to the soil. On the side, a rusting metal plate is flanked by specks of grey-green cladonia lichen. A thick carpet of moss on top is damp to the touch. At one end of the beam, it forms an understorey to a forest of tiny toadstools. Our inspection of this decaying piece of industrial archaeology is interrupted by a rattling sound, and we look up to see a streak of lights below the distant hill. The London–Edinburgh railway is a constant reminder of the competitor that brought the canal's demise. Ironically, it needed a parliamentary measure known as a Navigation Act to end the waterway's commercial life after little more than a century.

Derek Niemann

The century complete
❧ MARCH 2004 ❧

For several days, smoke palls have hung over parts of the forest. This is the month when most of the burning off is done. Some days in advance, the brushwood cutters have mown fire breaks. Roadside warning signs advise that controlled burning is to be expected. Late on a cold afternoon, I set out from Abbots Well, and dropped down Windmill Hill to Latchford Bottom. Beyond the valley, smoke rose to merge with the grey, overhanging sky. Winter feed had been strewn across Latchford Shade on the valley side. A few ponies were already enjoying it, but word was spreading; 16 ponies, with tails flying, raced across the valley line astern for their share of the banquet. Within a few minutes, others had joined them at a more sedate pace. Together, they packed in the calories to give warmth for another freezing night. A few small birds flitted among the gorse. Two murders of crows, some 15 in all, worked over the ground where the ponies had been. Their pecking suggested that they, too, had found a late afternoon feast. The path back was strewn with the decaying fragments of gorse branches, reminders that once this area, too, had been ablaze.

Graham Long

A mind full of story
❧ NOVEMBER 2005 ☙

Alone, I pace the springy turf of a green path leading up from Llyn Tecwyn Isaf into the northern Rhinogydd. These are the most wild and strange hills in the whole mountainous land of Wales. Ifor Williams, in his standard work *Enwau Lleoedd*, 'Names of Places', has the meaning as an elision of *yr hiniog* – the threshold – and I never come here without an encroaching sense of something otherworldly about them. Today, splashing on into the mist, the unremitting rain falling, I focus on the close particularities of place: the drop-beaded red blades of moor-grass; mist-wraiths' disorientating swirl; a ring-cairn alongside the track. Within this enclosed horizon there are soft mutterings on the wind of the sounds half-heard and the movement glimpsed only at the corner of an eye. And memories too – of a day long gone with my son Will, seven years old and clinging close in nervous apprehension of what might inhabit here, his mind full of story . . . The old way curves round above a morass to join the ancient trackway that climbs in from the south-west. A quick breeze roams in from that direction, lifts the skirts of the clouds and hustles them away. Suddenly, outlined on the crest of a bluff, Bryn Cader Faner stands stark and clear. Crown-like, stones pointing outwards, it has an intimate majesty perfectly in harmony with the cyclopean masonry of its setting. Four thousand years old, its artistry and mystery still impress. But less so than formerly, and from fewer angles. Soldiers on exercise in the Second World War destroyed much of it. The desecrated stones still lie scattered about. The Ministry of Defence, in reparation, should carefully restore them. I wonder if it ever will?

Jim Perrin

A fox's refuge

ꙮ DECEMBER 2005 ꙮ

In drenching weather I stood on the footbridge in the Tanat valley below Pistyll Rhaiadr, highest of Welsh waterfalls. The little river was plunging directly on to the mysterious natural arch below the main cataract. Its water was tinged with peat so that the whole fall had the colour of heavy flaxen hair. I turned to climb the path through the wood. Chaffinches flitted around, and the leaves of beech and birch were pale lemon, burnt orange, even a crinkled and glossy green. Beyond the first of the ancient cairns in the long valley above the fall, bracken had died back, revealing the landscape features. A harsh, insistent north wind whipped the rain into my face as I splashed along the sedgy, miry path. Under a louring sky, I reached the identifying outcrop, scanned the hillside beyond for the rocks, and there, slowly emergent from vegetation laid low by oncoming winter and rain, the stone row that leads to the stone circle of Rhos y Beddau – the moor of the graves. Suddenly, a shaft of sunlight seeded the rushes with diamonds, the whole landscape gleamed. As I walked back down the long valley, a double rainbow arched and the sun itself rolled along the ridge westerly. Above the waterfall once more, a dark dog fox loped round the shoulder of the moor, leapt the wall into the plantation of larch and Scots pine, made for the stream and waded for 20 yards before slipping across to the crest of rimming crags. Seconds later a pack of baying hounds poured over the wall, splashed through the water and streamed over the hill, aimless and off the scent. As for the fox, I suspect he had padded soft along the perilous ledge behind the fall, and, scentless, now squatted on his haunches, tongue lolling, and the water falling in front of him protectively.

Jim Perrin

The road to the Last Inn
JANUARY 2006

It has been more than 40 years since trains ran along the Mawddach estuary from Dolgellau to Barmouth but, fortunately, the track bed remains. The path runs first across lightly wooded fenland opening out to show Cadair Idris, edged with frost, rising above cold winter pastures. To the north, reed beds stretch across the valley almost to the foot of the opposing hills, Y Garn and Diffwys. At Penmaenpool, once home to a modest boat-building trade, a robust wooden toll bridge offers a short cut across the valley. This morning it is silent apart from a band of geese grazing noisily and the sound of energetic hammering from the old signal box – now an RSPB outpost. Further west, dry-stone walls built of large water-rounded cobbles curve up into the ancient birch woods. The hills close in from the south, and the track occupies a stone-clad embankment between the steep, wooded hillside and the tidal marshes. The tide is rising fast, driving curlew and oystercatchers ahead of it towards the track. Dark brown water sluices audibly between the fingers of marsh; bubbles of trapped air bursting like rainfall on the water surface. A sweeping curve leads up to the long bridge across the mouth of the estuary. Here, the Cambrian Coast railway line still crosses the Mawddach – sharing the wooden trestle with the footpath. Looking back inland, into the bitter east wind, the hills and sky are merging into the grey January dusk. But ahead, the light is on outside the Last Inn on the edge of Barmouth.

John Gilbey

Old grey stones
APRIL 2006

The ethereal beauty of the Lakes during the heavy snowfalls of late has had to be seen to be believed. Tracks everywhere across the hills have attested to the many attracted by their sparkle. Also making tracks are the drystone walls which also walk the fells — literally. The signs of their progression are not so much bootprints in the snow as the sudden wall gaps that appear each winter, courtesy of the hard frosts that freeze the ground and hoist walls fractionally upwards. Come the thaw, and given any weakness, they will 'rush'. Accommodating the vagaries of these 'grey millipedes on slow stone hooves', as poet Norman Nicholson described them, are the wallers — well aware of a wall's ability to shift with every hard snap, earth tremor or landslip and yet remain standing. So it was that Steve Allen found himself recently in heavy snow, fingers numbed and face reddened by the wind, walling at the English Nature reserve of Great Asby Scar with its limestone pavements. Allen has all the signs of his trade: a blood blister under an index fingernail; a radio relaying the fortunes of Carlisle United. A two-times gold winner for his walling at the Chelsea Flower Show and a frequent visitor to America to build sculptor Andy Goldsworthy creations, Allen knows his achievements count for little in these blasted uplands. He appears and disappears behind the wall, stooping to sort, select, discard and finally choose a cobble, then straightens his 6ft-something frame to see if it will fit in place. He builds the walls as they used to be built — in this case since 1763, a date he discovered chiselled on a bedrock stone while 'gapping' walls here. That was the year the British defeated Chief Pontiac's native Americans and still the world has not changed.

Tony Greenbank

ENVOI

When the coffee-pot was dry and the last pipe snuffed at the Country Diary writers' lunch in 1974, the *Guardian*'s editor Alistair Hetherington got up to thank his assorted guests before they caught their trains and buses back to Keswick, Plumgarth, Wilmslow, Charlburg, Whalton, Peebles and Surlingham. 'You contribute an element of sanity, even of humanity, to the paper every day,' he said. 'I hope we meet again, in something less than seventy years' time.'

Ted Ellis promptly beamed back: 'Ah, you'll have a new lot by then,' and – with the exception of Colin Luckhurst, who writes as vigorously as ever – he has been proved right. All the rest of that company are in their graves. But there was also truth in what Hetherington said in reply: 'Oh, I don't know. You last very well.' From Helena Swanwick, who was diarying aged 76, to Harry Griffin, who died in harness at 93, many *Guardian* Country Diary writers have worked far beyond the usual span.

A measure of their dedication is given in this final entry from Bill Campbell – final in terms of this book; he continued to write weekly until 23 November 1994 when he died at home on the day that people were reading his last contribution. He makes no bones about why he set out in the wheelchair to which he was confined after a car accident to search for a lethal poison. And what stopped him from taking it.

Deadly nightshade
❧ NOVEMBER 1992 ❧

I have always endeavoured, in these weekly pieces, to be meticulously truthful, so several times (in more mobile pre-accident days) I have left my typewriter and gone to the Forest to confirm that something was in bloom, in song, or on the wing; I therefore (being stumped for a theme) have no reservation in describing a recent train of thought which occurred in the intermediate state between consciousness and sleep. I decided that life was no longer worth living, particularly in view of the neglected state of my garden which was once voted equal first as the best kept in our little town, and the fact that I could no longer visit the usual sites, either by foot or by car, for inspiration for my Diaries. The most appropriate remedy (in the absence of sleeping pills, which I do not possess) seemed to be the berries of a plant which was the subject of my introduction to the Linnean system of plant nomenclature; for over eighty years ago, Dad had very firmly pointed it out to me, deadly nightshade. Having decided that, by some means or other, I would get a botanical friend to take me to the site (provided that the apparently immune pheasants and blackbirds had not scoffed the berries first), I was suddenly pulled up by a thought – but what about your *Guardian* piece which you have to write tomorrow? And so the final solution came to naught. Many letters from readers supplied flattering encouragement to carry on and, above all, so did the arrival next day of two of my converts to an interest in natural history in their teenages about forty years ago, to spend several hours digging and cleaning a weedy plot. Since I write this on my eighty-seventh birthday, having received many letters and cards, phone calls and visitors, I have to realise that life is still worth living.

W.D. Campbell

THE DIARISTS, 1904–2006

Page numbers refer to diary entries.

Rev. Graham Long, United Reformed Church minister, writer and mollusc specialist, 218

Phil Gates, senior lecturer in Botany at Durham University, 193, 205

John Thompson, insurance underwriter, 202

Pete Bowler, environmentalist, politician and shit-stirrer, 206, 209, 213

Jim Perrin, mountaineer and author, 219, 220

Richard Mabey, writer and environmentalist, 205

Jack Abbott, managing director of parcel-delivery business, 184

Ray Collier, forester and writer, 15, 192

Philip Price, teacher, 216

Peter Stowe, insurance broker, 214

Derek Niemann, RSPB youth magazines editor, 217

John Gilbey, writer and photographer, 221

Tony Greenbank, climber and journalist, 221

SELECT BIBLIOGRAPHY

These are all collections of *Guardian* country diaries, some with additional material.

Boyd, A.W., *The Country Diary of a Cheshire Man* (Collins, 1946)

Cocker, Mark, *A Tiger in the Sand* (Jonathan Cape, 2006)

Collier, Ray, *Highland Country Diaries* (Colin Baxter, 1997)

Condry, William, *A Welsh Country Diary* (Gomer, 1993)

Griffin, A. Harry, *A Lakeland Mountain Diary* (Crowood Press, 1990)

——— *A Lifetime of Mountains* (Aurum Press/Guardian, 2005)

Harper, Clifford, *Country Diary Drawings* (Agraphia Press, 2003)

Jackson, Mary and Ken (eds) *W.D. Campbell: Naturalist and Teacher* (The Wychwood Press, 2003)

Page, Jeannette (ed.), *A Country Diary* (Guardian/Fourth Estate, 1994)

Poyntz, Sarah, *A Burren Journal* (Tir Eolas, 2005)

Redfern, Roger, *A Guardian Peak District Diary* (Sigma, 1992)

—— *A Snowdonia Country Diary* (Gwasg Carreg Gwalch, 2004)

White, John T., *A Country Diary – Kent* (Cassell, 1974)

Wilson, Enid J., *Enid J. Wilson's Country Diary* (Hodder & Stoughton, 1988)